Study Guide and PSI Manual for Rubin and McNeil's

The Psychology of Being Human

Study Guide and PSI Manual for Rubin and McNeil's

The Psychology of Being Human

THIRD EDITION

TERRY MAUL
San Bernardino Valley College

RICHARD McGLYNN
Texas Tech University

1817

HARPER & ROW, PUBLISHERS, New York
Cambridge, Philadelphia, San Francisco,
London, Mexico City, São Paulo, Sydney

Sponsoring Editor: Kathy Whalen
Senior Project Editor: Karla B. Philip
Designer: Gayle Jaeger
Production Manager: Jeanie Berke
Compositor: Lexigraphics, Inc.
Printer and Binder: The Murray Printing Company

STUDY GUIDE AND PSI MANUAL for Rubin and McNeil's
THE PSYCHOLOGY OF BEING HUMAN, Third Edition

ISBN 0-06-044307-3

Contents

PART THREE: LEARNING AND THINKING

PART FOUR: FACING LIFE'S CHALLENGES

PART FIVE: DEVELOPMENT THROUGH LIFE

PART SIX: DISORDER AND THERAPY

PART SEVEN: RELATING TO ONE ANOTHER

Preface

If previous student experience is any indication of what you can hope for, a study guide such as this will noticeably improve your understanding of the material in the text and, as a result, will improve your performance on classroom examinations and your satisfaction with the course. This *Study Guide and PSI Manual,* designed to accompany *The Psychology of Being Human,* Third Edition, by Zick Rubin and Elton B. McNeil, provides you with open-ended PSI (Personalized System of Instruction) study questions, a Programmed Review Unit with answers, and two Self-Quizzes with answers, for each chapter in the Rubin/McNeil text. The open-ended study questions and Programmed Review Units focus on the important material of the text, helping you to organize your study and achieve a high level of understanding in less time. The Self-Quizzes, as well as the Programmed Review Units, will give you immediate feedback and, with corrections of mistakes, will thoroughly prepare you for classroom examinations on the text. Both the review materials and the Self-Quizzes are comprehensive, and the Self-Quizzes contain test items that are similar, in both format and material covered, to items that are likely to appear on a quiz that your instructor might give.

We recommend that you use this *Study Guide and PSI Manual* in either of two ways: 1) If your instructor uses the PSI approach (described in the Introduction to PSI) or if you want to understand the material particularly well, we recommend that you go through the material in the *Study Guide and PSI Manual* from beginning to end within the chapter that corresponds to the chapter you are reading in the Rubin/McNeil text. 2) Or, if the PSI method is not used, you can skip directly to the Programmed Review Unit in the appropriate chapter of the *Study Guide and PSI Manual.* You will find the Programmed Review Units to be most helpful if you read the chapter in *The Psychology of Being Human* before working on the Programmed Review Unit.

When you are reading the Programmed Review Unit for a chapter, be sure to do two things: 1) cover the answers in the margin with your hand or a piece of paper so that there is no way you can see the answer in advance, and 2) *write* the missing answer(s) in all the blank spaces in the sentence you are reading. Do not just try to *think* of the answer because studies show that active involvement leads to better retention. After writing your answer(s), get immediate feedback by uncovering the answer(s) in the margin before going on to the next sentence. This way you can circle any incorrect answers before going on to the next sentence. This will help you determine what part of the Rubin/McNeil text you need to restudy.

Both the open-ended study questions and the Programmed Review Unit sentences are accompanied by a page reference (in parentheses) in which this material can be found in *The Psychology of Being Human,* Third Edition.

Try to take the Self-Quizzes as though they were the in-class quizzes—and you will probably do better on the actual classroom tests. You can get valuable practice in reading a quiz question carefully, circling the single best answer for each question, and making sure you answer all of the questions; each of these three considerations is frequently overlooked, which unnecessarily lowers a student's quiz score. After completing each Self-Quiz, you can immediately check to see how many of your answers were correct and then restudy any material the quiz indicates you may not have fully understood.

Terry Maul
Richard McGlynn

Introduction to PSI

If the course you are taking is being taught by the Personalized System of Instruction (PSI), it is likely to be organized around a few basic principles of learning which have only recently been systematically applied to higher education. Although there are many variations, PSI courses usually include dividing the course material into manageable blocks or units, requiring a high level of mastery on each block, allowing the student to determine his or her own rate of progress, and permitting repeated testing without penalty until mastery is achieved. Since the consistent length of the chapters in *The Psychology of Being Human,* Third Edition, is ideal for a PSI course, this guide is organized around the chapter as the basic unit. If you follow the guide you will be doing all the things that an *A* student would do in studying any textbook. In PSI courses the goal is usually complete mastery of each chapter, or in other words, *A*-level performance.

Most PSI courses include frequent testing and self-pacing. This means that, at least to some degree, you determine (with the help of the guide) when you are ready to take a test on a chapter. Because the study questions are designed to prepare you for the chapter test, you should be able to demonstrate mastery on the test. However, if your performance is not at the level required, you are given corrective feedback and allowed to take another test on the chapter after restudying.

The real essence of a PSI course from the student's point of view may be the precise specification of what is to be learned. That is the function of the study questions. You will not have to wonder what is going to be on a test because the study questions tell you. When you are able to answer the open-ended study questions for a chapter, you should be able to answer the test questions even if they are multiple-choice questions, because the test questions are based directly on the study questions.

For each chapter of *The Psychology of Being Human,* Third Edition, this guide contains a number of study questions which follow the textbook closely. For each succeeding paragraph or section, these questions ask you to define, describe, summarize, and list, in such a way that if you follow the guide you will have studied everything you need to know to demonstrate mastery of the chapter on a chapter test. The short Self-Quizzes after the initial study questions and the Programmed Review Unit will give you a chance to demonstrate your understanding to yourself before you take a chapter test at the hands of your instructor or an assistant.

The guide is designed to encourage you to master each chapter at a high level. If your past academic success convinces you that your study habits are superior, you will probably be doing all the things the guide encourages anyway. In that case the guide can best serve you as a mechanism to review before each test. However, we found that most students can profit from the guide if it is used properly:

1. Look over the study questions just enough to know what the chapter is about. Then read the chapter.

2. Write the answers to the study questions in the guide by following along in the text. Your answers should consist of short phrases rather than complete sentences. Make your answers as accurate as possible, but do not copy the answer out of the text. Pay careful attention to exactly what each question asks you to do. By keeping your answers short and doing just what is required to answer each question, you can make the most efficient use of the study questions. There should be enough space provided with each question for the kinds of short answers we have in mind. If your handwriting is large, use extra sheets of paper.

3. Go back over the study questions and *actively* study your answers. The most efficient way to learn and remember the material is to make sure that you *understand* both the study questions and the answers to them. If you try to use rote memory for all the material in the chapter, you will face an overwhelming task, and the results may well be frustrating.

4. All the while you should be testing your retention, but do not use the Self-Quizzes provided until you have convinced yourself that you have mastered the chapter. At that point, if you get all the items on the Self-Quiz correct, you should be ready for the chapter test. If some of your answers are not correct, it means that you probably need some more review. Start with the study questions that correspond to the items you missed on the Self-Quiz. As you move through the chapters you should depend more and more on your own testing of your retention and less and less on the Self-Quizzes.

5. Your instructor and assistants are valuable resources. If there is something that you do not understand after thorough study, get help from someone on the teaching staff before you take the chapter test.

If you have really mastered the chapter, you should pass the chapter test. However, when you miss some items on a chapter test you can learn something from the experience by using the feedback provided. Each item on a PSI test is referenced by the number of a particular study guide question so you will know exactly which questions to review. In other words, you know the ones you missed even though you probably will not be allowed to look at the test again. This kind of immediate feedback greatly facilitates learning, but it can only work if you look up the study questions right after the test. The smart way to use the feedback from a test is to note not only what you missed, but how many you missed. The PSI multiple-choice tests that accompany this guide will test your mastery in relation to the study questions. The test questions are necessarily limited in testing your broad understanding of *The Psychology of Being Human,* but if you have studied efficiently enough to answer such a wide variety of questions, we can be confident that you have grasped the broader issues.

You can expect things to get easier and go faster the more chapters you master. One reason for this is that the testing situation should become more of a challenge and less of a threat as time passes. Second, if you use the guide wisely on the first few chapters, you should come to depend on it less with each succeeding chapter as your confidence in your own study skills increases. In addition, having mastered the earlier chapters of *The Psychology of Being Human,* Third Edition, you will have a better background for reading the later chapters. Although you might feel very frustrated if you run into a chapter that seems impossible to master even after several attempts at the chapter tests, you can be comforted by the knowledge that this happens to even the best of students in PSI courses and that things will almost certainly improve in the next chapter.

Finally, both teachers and students really share the responsibility for the outcome of a PSI course, and the result is that they become involved in a relationship that can be mutually satisfying. That has been the case in our own experience with PSI; we hope it is yours.

Study Guide and PSI Manual for Rubin and McNeil's

The Psychology of Being Human

Chapter 1

What Is Psychology?

1. What is the nature of the questions psychologists ask? How do they differ from the questions we all try to answer in our everyday lives? (page 4)

2. Define psychology. What is the purpose of psychology? When did it develop? (6)

3. *BOX 1:* Identify the following in the history of psychology: (6)

Aristotle—

John Locke—

Tabula rasa—

Wilhelm Wundt—

Structuralism—

Functionalism—

John B. Watson—

Behaviorism—

Freud—

4. *BOX 1:* How has the subject matter of psychology changed in the last 10 to 15 years? (6)

THE RESEARCH ADVENTURE

5. What are the usual settings for psychological research? Can it be done elsewhere? (8)

6. What did the parable of the Good Samaritan suggest to Darley and Batson about helping behavior? (9)

7. Describe the setting for the Good Samaritan study and the six experimental conditions. (9)

8. Summarize the results of the Good Samaritan study in terms of the two variables investigated (hurry and topic). What general conclusions about helping behavior can be drawn from this experiment? (11)

9. Define flashbulb memory. What were Brown and Kulik's two hypotheses about flashbulb memories? Define hypothesis. (12)

10. How did Brown and Kulik test their hypotheses about flashbulb memories? Summarize the results. (13)

11. What is Brown and Kulik's speculation about the origin of our ability to form flashbulb memories? (14)

12. List five sources of ideas for psychological research. What is meant by the cumulative process of scientific research? (14)

13. Define theory. What two things do theories do for psychologists? (16)

THE METHODS OF PSYCHOLOGY

14. Summarize the two principal characteristics of all psychological research and contrast them with personal experience. (16)

15. What two factors often dictate the psychologist's choice of a sample? Identify the problems with using college students as subjects. (17)

16. What determines the degree to which the results of research can be generalized from one group of people to another? Define case study. (18)

17. List four reasons for using animals as subjects. (19)

18. List the three kinds of measures psychologists use. Define survey. How did Rubin measure romantic love? (19)

19. List the major advantage and two disadvantages of laboratory research. (21)

20. Describe the two types of descriptive studies. What is the major disadvantage of this research strategy? (22)

21. Define correlational study. Why is it true that "correlation does not imply causation"? (22)

22. Define: (23)

Experiment—

Independent variable—

Dependent variable—

Experimental group—

Control group—

Statistically significant difference—

23. *BOX 3:* Define experimenter expectancy effects. Summarize Rosenthal's study. How do expectancy effects work? How can they be controlled? (25)

RESEARCH AND APPLICATION

24. Describe and distinguish each of the following: (26)

Basic research—

Applied research—

Practice of psychology—

SUBFIELDS OF PSYCHOLOGY

25. Identify the following subfields of psychology: (27)

Experimental—

Clinical, counseling, school, community—

Personnel, organizational, engineering, consumer—

Developmental, educational—

Personality and social—

26. *BOX 4:* Where do most psychologists work? Summarize the differences between psychiatrists and clinical psychologists. (27)

PSYCHOLOGICAL ISSUE: *PARASCIENCE*

27. Define: (33)

Phrenology—

Graphology—

Biorhythms—

Astrology—

28. What is the psychological appeal of parascience? (37)

Self-Quiz

1. Your text describes psychology as:
- **a.** the study of mental health.
- **b.** the science of behavior and mental processes.
- **c.** the science of the mind.
- **d.** the experimental research method. (Study Question 2)

2. Darley and Batson used the parable of the Good Samaritan to:
- **a.** illustrate ideal human behavior.
- **b.** teach subjects helping behavior.
- **c.** investigate the effects of religion on behavior.
- **d.** suggest variables which affect helping behavior. (Study Question 6)

3. The concept of unconscious motivation was emphasized by:
- **a.** Locke.
- **b.** Wundt.
- **c.** Watson.
- **d.** Freud. (Study Question 3)

4. Behaviorists insist that the proper subject matter of psychology is:
- **a.** conscious processes.
- **b.** thinking.
- **c.** any behavior that is observable.
- **d.** behavior that is both observable and of practical importance. (Study Question 3)

5. Which of the following is *not* commonly used in psychological research?
- **a.** The subjective method.
- **b.** The case study.

c. The experimental method.
d. The survey method. (Study Question 14)

6. In measuring the specific aspects of behavior that they are most interested in, psychologists record:
a. overt behavior.
b. physiological responses.
c. self-reports.
d. all of the above. (Study Question 18)

7. The correlational method does *not* tell us about:
a. causation.
b. relationships among variables.
c. survey results.
d. the behavior of animals and humans. (Study Question 21)

8. An educational psychologist does an experiment to test a new method of teaching reading. One class uses the new method and another similar class uses the old. In this experiment, the group using the old method is the:
a. experimental group.
b. dependent group.
c. control group.
d. independent group. (Study Question 22)

9. A difference between a psychiatrist and a clinical psychologist is:
a. the psychiatrist has an M.D.; the clinical psychologist does not.
b. the psychiatrist diagnoses disturbances; the clinical psychologist treats them.
c. the clinical psychologist diagnoses disturbances; the psychiatrist treats them.
d. a psychiatrist's clients are disturbed people; a clinical psychologist's clients think they are disturbed, but they are not. (Study Question 26)

10. Biorhythm theory is based on:
a. experimentally tested hypotheses.
b. the scientific method.
c. graphology.
d. none of the above. (Study Question 27)

Answers to Self-Quiz: 1.b 2.d 3.d 4.c 5.a 6.d 7.a 8.c 9.a 10.d

Programmed Review Unit

behavior
mental

1. To start with basics, psychology is the science of ________ and ________ processes, especially among humans. (6)

shaping

2. Psychologists try to provide better answers to personal questions and to help people make use of these answers in ________ their lives. (6)

THE RESEARCH ADVENTURE

Answers	Items
63 10 Fifty-three 29	**3.** In Darley and Batson's Good Samaritan study, ________ percent of the no-hurry subjects offered help, while only ________ percent of the big-hurry subjects helped the victim. ________ percent of the divinity students preparing to give a talk about the parable of the Good Samaritan offered aid to the victim, compared to ________ percent of those who were preparing to talk about nonreligious topics. (11)
situations people	**4.** A great deal of research is currently being conducted on both the sorts of ________ that elicit helping behavior and the sorts of ________ who are likely to be helpful. (11)
flashbulb setting	**5.** According to Brown and Kulik, ________ memories are not memories for an historical event itself but rather enduring memories of the ________ and manner in which a person heard of the event. (12)
hypothesis	**6.** An ________ is an educated guess. (13)
most importance	**7.** Brown and Kulik found that ________ people had flashbulb memories, and there was clear evidence for the link that had been hypothesized between the personal ________ of an event and flashbulb memories. (13)
unanswered	**8.** Just why we are likely to form flashbulb memories for sudden and impactful events remains an ________ question. (14)
sensory conscious observable	**9.** All knowledge, Locke believed, derives from ________ encounters with the physical world. In contrast to Wundt and American students who were interested in ________ processes, John Watson and his followers asserted that the only proper subject matter for psychology was ________ behavior. (16)
experiences obedience	**10.** Our personal ________ are one of the most important sources of research questions in psychology. Another source of ideas are news events. Milgram's research on people's ________ to authority was inspired by the horrors of the Nazi era. (14)
problems	**11.** Research is often prompted by the desire to find ways of solving pressing psychological and social ________. (14)
theory	**12.** A set of concepts and hypotheses that fit together to provide a perspective on some aspect of the world is called a ________. (16)

THE METHODS OF PSYCHOLOGY

Answers	Items
systematic objective	**13.** Psychologists strive to study behavior in ways that are ________ (based on a thorough and well-organized search for facts) and ________ (based on careful observations that different observers can agree on, rather than one person's intuitions). (16)
representative generalize me	**14.** Hopefully, the psychologist attempts to discover principles of human behavior by studying a ________ sample of humans so that it may be possible to ________ from the sample to a larger segment of society. When reading a psychological study be sure to ask, "Do their findings apply to ________?" (17)
patterns differences	**15.** Researchers are interested in common ________ and also individual ________. (18)

Clinical

16. ________ psychologists can often learn a great deal about personality from intensive case studies of individuals. (19)

learning

17. Much of what we know about human ________ is based on studies of parallel processes in pigeons, rats, and other animals. (19)

measuring
overt
stops
physiological
questions
survey

18. Psychologists must devise ways of observing and ________ those specific aspects of behavior that they are interested in. Sometimes the researcher will record aspects of a subject's ________ behavior, such as the number of times a baby smiles or whether a subject in the Good Samaritan study ________ to help the "victim." Researchers sometimes use special equipment to record a subject's ________ responses, such as heart rate or brain waves. And researchers use personal interviews, surveys, or tests of personality, intelligence, or ability or they record people's responses to ________ put to them. For example, the flashbulb memory study is a ________ in which subjects gave self-reports. (19)

trashcans

19. An investigator who wanted to find out how much liquor was being consumed in a town that was officially "dry" demonstrated an unobstrusive measurement strategy by counting empty liquor bottles in ________. (20)

facial expressions

20. Experimenter expectancy effects may be caused by subtle nonverbal cues such as ________ ________ and tone of voice, which can provide signals to the subject as to what response is expected. (25)

eye

21. Rubin found that the more the members of couples indicated they loved each other (via an attitude scale), the more ________ contact they tended to have. (21)

generalize

22. Because the laboratory is an artificial environment, it is sometimes difficult to ________ from the ways subjects behave in the lab to the ways they would behave in other situations. (21)

description
observation
interviews
cannot

23. When a researcher is engaged in ________, he or she is primarily concerned with setting forth a clear account of the subject's behavior or self-reports. Descriptive studies include ________ studies and ________ which are illustrated by watching nursery-school children and asking people to describe experience of loss, respectively. A good description of behavior ________ tell us why it is happening. (22)

control
effects
relationship

24. An experiment is a study in which the researcher exerts direct ________ over some aspect of the subjects' environment and then the researcher assesses the ________. In a correlational study, such as the flashbulb memory study, the researcher tries to discover the ________ between two or more aspects of people's behavior, attitudes, or background. (23)

variables
causes

25. Just because two measures (or ________) are related does not in itself tell us what ________ what to occur. (23)

chance

26. A statistically significant difference is one that is highly unlikely to have come about by ________ and therefore can be attributed to the impact of your experimental treatments. (24)

independent

27. In experiments, the variable that the researcher has control over is called the ________ variable. (24)

experimental

28. The group of subjects who receive the special treatment is called the ________ group. The control group plays a vital function in the experiment by ruling out the effects of extraneous factors on the

dependent
experiment

________________ variable. The Good Samaritan study was an example of an ________________. (24)

RESEARCH AND APPLICATION

basic
Applied
application

29. The purpose of ________________ research is to advance our understanding of behavior without any immediate concern for the practical uses of this understanding, although in the long run it may prove to be of great practical importance. ________________ research, on the other hand, is work that attempts, from the outset, to help solve a practical problem. The practice of psychology is the direct ________________ of psychological knowledge. (26)

SUBFIELDS OF PSYCHOLOGY

Experimental
commercial or industrial
death
Clinical
psychiatrists

30. ________________ psychologists do research on the most fundamental psychological processes, such as perception, learning, memory, motivation, and emotion. Personnel, organizational, and consumer psychologists generally work in ________________ settings. Developmental psychologists are concerned with the development of human capacities, beginning with conception and ending with ________________. (27)

31. ________________ psychologists, who are Ph.D.s, more often use psychological tests and are more likely to draw on theory and history of illnesses than are ________________, who, because they are M.D.s, are able to make use of drugs and other medical treatments. (28)

PSYCHOLOGICAL ISSUE: *PARASCIENCE*

facts
bumps
graphology
larger
negative
negative

32. The authors of the text urge you to retain a healthy respect for the search for ________________, as opposed to unsubstantiated claims. (33)

33. Phrenologists believe that they need only to measure head ________________ to determine the shape of the brain and diagnose the subject's personality. (33)

34. The authors believe that ________________ is more of an art than a science and that it is not an art that is likely to yield particularly accurate results. Zweigenhaft (1977) suggests that the more confident people feel about themselves, the ________________ their signatures tend to be. (34)

35. Evidence from scientific studies of biorhythms has been uniformly ________________. Systematic attempts by psychologists to check out astrological predictions have repeatedly yielded ________________ results. (36)

Self-Quiz

1. Psychology is currently defined as:
a. the study of the soul.
b. the science of behavior and mental processes.

c. the study of conscious processes.
d. the science of the mind.

2. Psychologists do all but which one of the following?
a. Try to provide better answers to personal questions.
b. Try to help people to shape their lives.
c. Try to read people's minds.
d. Try to be scientific.

3. The setting for psychological research is likely to be:
a. hospitals.
b. highways.
c. the local bar.
d. all of the above.

4. Which one of the following was *not* found in the Good Samaritan study?
a. Ninety-three percent of the no-hurry subjects offered help to the victims.
b. Ten percent of the big-hurry subjects offered help to the victims.
c. Fifty-three percent of the students thinking about the Good Samaritan offered help.
d. Twenty-nine percent of the students not thinking about the Good Samaritan offered help.

5. Which one of the following statements is false?
a. A hypothesis is a guess.
b. A theory is a set of ideas that provide a perspective on some aspect of the world.
c. A subjective finding is one that different observers can agree on.
d. Psychological research is often prompted by the desire to solve problems.

6. Which one of the following was *not* found by Brown and Kulik?
a. Most people have flushbulb memories.
b. There was a link between taking drugs and having flashbulb memories.
c. Flashbulb memories are not memories of the event itself but are memories of the setting and manner in which a person heard the event.
d. There was a link between personal importance and flashbulb memories.

7. Clinical psychologists are characterized by all but which one of the following?
a. They often treat mentally ill people with drugs.
b. They often use psychological tests to diagnose problems.
c. They are interested in the case history type of research.
d. They probably pursued graduate-school studies, and may have Ph.D.s.

8. Counting the number of empty liquor bottles in trashcans best demonstrates:
a. a systematic search procedure.
b. a subjective observation.

c. an unobstrusive observation.
d. proof that the owner of the trash can is a drinker.

9. Which statement is false?
   a. The independent variable is the one the researcher controls.
   b. The dependent variable may vary according to your experimental treatments.
   c. The control group receives the experimental treatments.
   d. Variables are measured observations.

10. Which statement about parascience is true?
    a. Phrenology is currently popular.
    b. One study showed that confident people have smaller signatures.
    c. There is no scientific evidence to support the existence of biorhythms.
    d. There is scientific evidence to support the accuracy of astrological predictions.

Answers: 1.b 2.c 3.d 4.a 5.c 6.b 7.a 8.c 9.c 10.d

Chapter 2

The Brain and Nervous System

THE NERVOUS SYSTEM

1. Identify the two main subdivisions of the nervous system. (39)

2. Locate, identify and distinguish. (40)

Afferent neurons—

Efferent neurons—

Association neurons—

3. Define reflex. Use the terms in the question above to explain how a reflex works. (40)

4. Distinguish between the two major divisions of the peripheral nervous system. (40)

5. What is the major difference between the sympathetic and parasympathetic nervous systems? List the specific opposite effects of each system. (Notice how these specific effects are naturally related to the different functions of the two systems.) (40)

6. Identify: (42)

Endocrine system—

Hormones—

Epinephrine—

7. Locate and identify: (43)

Neuron—

Cell body—

Axon—

Dendrite—

Direction of nerve impulse—

8. Define axonal transmission and the all-or-nothing principle. (43)

9. Define synaptic transmission and excitatory and inhibitory messages. Tell how synaptic transmission affects other neurons. (43)

10. *BOX 1:* List three differences between the brain and the computer. What functions are best suited for each? (44)

THE BRAIN

11. Describe the brain in cellular terms. How does the size of the brain compare to animal brains? (45)

12. How do each of the following techniques help us learn about the functioning of the brain? (45)

    Electrical stimulation—

    Brain damage—

    Brain surgery—

13. Describe brain waves and the electroencephalogram (EEG). How is the EEG used? (47)

14. Explain the use of these recent techniques to study the brain. (48)

    Microelectrodes—

    Blood-flow measurement—

15. *BOX 2:* Describe the stimoceiver and its current uses. How does electrical stimulation stop a bull in midcharge? (46)

16. Locate and list the four basic sets of structures of the brain. Compare the brain stem in humans and lower animals. (50)

17. Locate the medulla and the hypothalamus. Summarize their functions. (50)

18. Locate, summarize the functions of, and note the effects of damage to each of the following: (50)

Cerebellum—

Limbic system—

Amygdala—

Hippocampus—

19. Summarize the difference in the size and function of the cortex in humans versus lower animals. (51)

20. List, locate, and give the principal function of each of the four lobes of the cortex. (52)

21. Study Figure 2.9 carefully. What determines how much sensory and motor cortex is devoted to a particular body part? (54)

22. *BOX 3:* Define biofeedback. To what bodily functions has it been applied? How is biofeedback like learning to ride a bicycle? (49)

23. *BOX 3:* Summarize the results of Brown's biofeedback research, Orne and Wilson's study, and Sterman's application of biofeedback. (49)

24. Define aphasia. How does it help us to understand the specialization (localization) of brain function? (53)

25. Define and distinguish: (53)

Broca's aphasia—

Wernicke's aphasia—

Prosopagnosia—

26. What general principle of brain function emerges from studies of brain activity during silent reading, reading aloud, performing difficult mental tasks, and experiencing stress? Define reticular formation. (55)

27. How do transmitter substances excite or inhibit specific neurons in the brain? What are the effects of a deficiency or excess of dopamine? (56)

28. Define neuropeptides. List their various effects. (56)

OUR TWO BRAINS

29. Describe the functions controlled primarily by the right and left hemispheres in right- and left-handed people. Note the corresponding effects of damage to one hemisphere or the other. (57)

30. Define corpus callosum. When the corpus callosum is cut, what are the effects with respect to epilepsy, personality, and intelligence? (57)

31. Describe the Sperry-Gazzaniga experiments with split-brain patients. (58)

32. Describe the evidence for specialization of function of the two hemispheres. What important qualifications must be made concerning specialization? (58)

EFFECTS OF EXPERIENCE ON THE BRAIN

33. Summarize the method, results, and conclusions from Rosenzweig's experiment. (59)

34. *BOX 4:* List three effects of malnutrition on brain development. Also, note specifically the effects of consuming foods rich in lecithin and carbohydrates. (61)

PSYCHOLOGICAL ISSUE: *BIOLOGICAL RHYTHMS*

35. Define circadian rhythm. List the functions that follow a circadian rhythm. What rhythms are hardest to reestablish after experiencing "jet lag"? (65)

36. Define ultradian rhythm and summarize Chase's results. Define infradian rhythm. (67)

37. What is the evidence for Frank Brown's controversial position? Is there a link between the moon and human behavior? (68)

38. Summarize the effects of the seasons on happiness, suicide rates, and mental hospital admissions. (69)

Self-Quiz

1. The nerve which carries the sensation of burning from the finger to the brain is:
a. association.
b. efferent.
c. respondent.
d. afferent. (Study Question 2)

2. Increases in heart rate and respiration, and the slowing of digestion are all caused by the triggering of the:
a. sympathetic nervous system.
b. parasympathetic nervous system.
c. somatic nervous system.
d. sensorimotor nervous sytem. (Study Question 5)

3. The all-or-nothing principle of impulse transmission refers to:
a. only the functioning of the central nervous system.
b. the intensity threshold which determines if the neuron will fire.
c. the direction of nerve impulses.
d. only synaptic transmission. (Study Question 8)

4. The tiny gap between two nerve cells is called the:
a. myelin.
b. vesicle.
c. synapse.
d. transmitter. (Study Question 9)

5. The ball-like mass behind the brain stem which is concerned with coordination is:
a. the medulla.
b. the cerebellum.
c. the cerebral cortex.
d. the amygdala. (Study Question 18)

6. The visual cortex can be found in which lobe of the brain?
a. Frontal.

b. Temporal.
c. Parietal.
d. Occipital. (Study Question 20)

7. An individual with Wernicke's aphasia has:
   a. damaged frontal lobes.
   b. frequent lapses into periods of fantasy.
   c. inappropriate and nonsensical use of words.
   d. mental retardation. (Study Question 25)

8. When split-brain patients were asked to use their left hands to point to what they had seen, they pointed to:
   a. the part of the stimulus that was "seen" in the left hemisphere.
   b. the part of the stimulus that was "seen" in the right hemisphere.
   c. the entire stimulus.
   d. stimuli that had not been presented at all. (Study Question 31)

9. Malnutrition causes all but which of the following problems in brain development?
   a. Reduction in the number of cells in the cerebellum.
   b. Shrinkage in axons.
   c. Reduction in the number of synapses.
   d. Growth of dendritic spines. (Study Question 34)

10. An ultradian rhythm:
    a. completes a cycle every 24 hours.
    b. completes a cycle in less than 24 hours.
    c. completes a cycle in more than 24 hours.
    d. is a type of brain wave. (Study Question 36)

Answers to Self-Quiz: 1.d 2.a 3.b 4.c 5.b 6.d 7.c 8.b 9.d 10.b

Programmed Review Unit

THE NERVOUS SYSTEM

spinal cord
peripheral
sensory
motor

1. The central nervous system is made up of the brain and ________________ and is the place where information processing occurs. The ________________ nervous system contains two types of nerves: neurons that collect messages and transmit them *to* the spinal cord or brain (afferent or ________________ neurons) and neurons that carry messages *from* the brain or spinal cord to muscles and glands (efferent or ________________ neurons). (39)

connections
brain

2. Association neurons in the spinal cord make ________________ between incoming and outgoing messages. A reflex occurs without involving the ________________. (40)
3. The peripheral nervous system is subdivided into two parts: the

somatic **autonomic** **sympathetic** **frightened/parasympathetic** **opposite**	__________ nervous system, which controls voluntary muscles, and the __________ nervous system, which controls glands and involuntary muscles. The autonomic nervous system is further subdivided into two parts: the __________ nervous system, which is active when the body is responding to stress, as when a person is __________, and the __________ nervous system, which tells the organs to do the __________ of what the sympathetic division directs them to do. (40)
endocrine/hormones **epinephrine**	**4.** The autonomic nervous system affects the body by stimulating organs in the __________ system to produce __________. For example, the adrenal glands release __________, a hormone that helps activate the body in times of stress. (40)
body **dendrites** **axon**	**5.** A neuron consists of three principal parts: the cell __________, which contains the nucleus; the __________, which are many short fibers that project from the cell body and that receive activity from nearby cells; and the __________, a long fiber that extends away from one side of the cell body and transmits messages to other neurons or to muscles and glands. (43)
feet **thousandths**	**6.** A neuron in the spinal cord may have an axon two or three __________ long, whereas neurons in the brain may cover only a few __________ of an inch. (43)
dendrites/cell body **axon** **neuron/gland**	**7.** Nerve messages normally move in one direction—from the __________ and the __________, along the __________ to the dendrites or cell body of the next __________, or to a muscle or __________. (43)
two/axonal **synaptic**	**8.** Messages are transmitted through the nervous system in __________ ways. There is __________ transmission—the movement of nerve impulses along the surface of a neuron. And there is __________ transmission—the transfer of impulses *between* neurons. (43)
electrical **all-or-none**	**9.** Axonal transmission is primarily an __________ process. A neuron will only fire completely if the electrical impulse is strong enough; this is called the __________ principle. (43)
synapse **dendrites**	**10.** A microscopic gap, called the __________, separates the end of each terminal from the __________ or cell body of another neuron. (43)
transmitter **inhibit** **brain**	**11.** When an electrical nerve impulse reaches the end of the axon, it causes the release of a chemical __________ substance that crosses the synapse and gives a message to the next neuron. The message may either excite or __________ the firing of the next neuron. In the __________ it is common for one neuron to receive messages from hundreds of other neurons. (43)

THE BRAIN

slower **millions** **less** **unlikely**	**12.** In contrast to computers the human brain has a __________ rate of transmission, but information can be handled on __________ of channels in parallel rather than processing one message at a time. Also, the neurons of the brain are __________ reliable components, but the deletion of many neurons is __________ to make much

Answers	Items
flexible	difference. The brain's operations are also more ________ than those of a computer. (44)
nerve cells glial/nourishment three largest	13. The brain contains 100 billion ________ and ten times as many ________ cells which provide ________ and support for the nerve cells. The human brain weighs approximately ________ pounds, and in proportion to body weight, the human brain is the ________ of all brains. (45)
fluid	14. The brain is protected by several layers of membrane and cushioning ________. (45)
sensory/motor	15. Electrical stimulation of the brain has been used to determine locations for specific ________ and ________ functions. (47)
pain/epileptic	16. Electrical stimulation of the brain has helped persons to control ________, ________ seizures and spastic muscle contractions. (47)
blood stem limbic/cerebral	17. The more activity that occurs in a brain part, the more ________ will flow to that part. The human brain is composed of four basic sets of structures: the brain ________, cerebellum, ________ system, and ________ cortex. (48)
medulla heartbeat reflex hypothalamus eating sex emotion pleasure	18. At the bottom of the brain stem lies the ________, which controls such basic physical rhythms as ________ and breathing, as well as containing ________ centers for vomiting, sneezing, coughing, and swallowing. The ________ monitors automatic aspects of behavior, such as ________, drinking, ________, and sleeping. It also plays a direct role in patterns of ________, such as rage, terror, and ________. (50)
behind position motion	19. The cerebellum is positioned ________ the brain stem and is largely concerned with automatic controls of body ________ and ________. (50)
limbic amygdala emotional hippocampus	20. Only mammals have a ________ system, which is at the bottom of the cerebral cortex. Electrical stimulation or removal of one limbic structure, the ________, have opposite effects on an animal's ________ expressions. Another structure on the limbic system, the ________, appears to play a critical role in short-term memory. (50)
80 interpreted fissure/frontal time emotional parietal oriented occipital visual temporal hearing	21. The cerebral cortex takes up ________ percent of the human brain, and is the place where sensory impulses concerning sight, sound, taste, smell, and touch are ________. Ahead of the central ________ is the ________ lobe, which seems to contribute to our understanding of ________ and to be involved in ________ expression. Behind the central fissure is the ________ lobe, which helps keep us physically ________ in our environment. At the rear of the cerebral cortex is the ________ lobe, which interprets ________ information. Beneath another fissure lies the ________ lobe, which seems to be involved with ________, language, and memory. (51)
50	22. The hands and mouth make up only a small percentage of the volume of the body but they merit almost ________ percent of the motor cortex. (53)
Broca's	23. If damage occurs in a region of the frontal lobe called ________

aphasia	area, people will experience a type of language breakdown, or ________, that is characterized by poor articulation and faulty grammar. If damage occurs to Wernicke's area, in the left
temporal	________ lobe, pronunciation and grammar are normal but
inappropriate or nonsensical	the words chosen are often ________. Prosopagrosia is the
faces	inability to identify people from their ________, and is caused
occipital	by damage on the underside of both ________ lobes. (53)
300,000	**24.** In the United States each year, approximately ________ people suffer strokes when the blood vessels leading to their brains are
fat	blocked by ________ deposits, or when a clot forms in an
bursts/brain	artery, or when an artery ________. Once ________ tissue is destroyed, it cannot be regenerated. (55)
waves	**25.** Biofeedback can be used to monitor and alter brain ________,
beat/pressure	heart ________, blood ________ and muscle
contractions	________. Subjects showing alpha waves may report the state
pleasant/unpleasant	as either ________ or ________. (49)
	26. Brown found that while in the beta state many of the subjects reported
worry/fear	feelings of ________, anger, ________, and
theta	excitement. In the more mysterious and rare ________ state, only a few of the people could identify definite feelings, although eight subjects indicated that their minds were involved in some sort of
problem solving	________. Delta waves are characteristic of deep
sleep/infant	________ or the ________ mind. (47)
epileptics	**27.** Some studies show that biofeedback has helped ________ to overcome a deficiency in a pattern of brain waves called the sensorimotor
four	rhythm. When we read silently, at least ________ areas of the brain are activated, including the occipital lobe and Broca's area in the
frontal	________ lobe. (47)
30	**28.** About ________ different types of proteinlike molecules are known or are suspected to be chemical transmitters in the brain. Among the best known are dopamine, norepinephrine, and
serotonin/dopamine	________. An excess of ________ in the limbic system is now believed to be a cause of hallucinations and other disruptions of thought and emotion that characterize
schizophrenia	________. (55)
	29. In the family of natural brain chemicals called neuropeptides,
endorphine	enkephaline and ________ have the ability to reduce
pain	________. These chemicals also occur in emotional centers,
amygdala	such as the ________, where they serve to keep our moods under control. (56)

OUR TWO BRAINS

right	**30.** The ________ side of the brain controls the left side of the
left	body, and vice versa. In right-handed people, the ________ hemisphere has primary control over linguistic abilities, such as
reading/writing	speaking, ________, and ________, whereas the other hemisphere has primary control over nonverbal skills, including
musical	________ ability, recognition of complex visual problems, and
emotion	the expression and recognition of ________. In left-handers,
evenly	these functions seem to be more ________ distributed between

left

the two hemispheres. Patients with lesions to the ________________ side of their brain feel depressed, whereas patients with lesions in the other side do not. (57)

corpus callosum
epilepsy
successful

31. The two hemispheres are connected by the ________________, which transfers information received by one half of the brain over to the other half. Brain surgeons have cut the corpus callosum of some people afflicted with uncontrollable ________________ in hopes of confining seizures to one hemisphere. This type of operation has proved to be ________________. (57)

Ninety-four
left

32. ________________ percent of us are right-handed. People pay more attention to the ________________ side of another person's face becuase their right hemisphere is more skilled in analyzing faces. (58)

left
before/left

33. In some cases, if linguistic abilites are lost because of damage in the ________________ hemisphere, the other hemisphere can take over these functions. This is more likely to be true if the damage occurs ________________ age eight or if the person is ________________ handed, because specialization of hemispheres seems to be less extensive in these people. (59)

EFFECTS OF EXPERIENCE ON THE BRAIN

chemical

34. Scientists believe that what we learn or remember is probably reflected in either physical or ________________ changes in the brain. (59)

cerebellum
axons
physical/intellectual
acetylcholine
sleep

35. One effect of malnutrition is to reduce the number of brain cells in the ________________, the portion of the brain responsible for fine motor control and coordination. Another effect is on the quality of nerve cell parts: ________________ in malnourished animals shrink in diameter in many parts of the brain. Tests on undernourished children show them to be retarded in many ________________ and ________________ skills. Foods, such as soybeans, which are rich in lecithin, can increase the amount of ________________, a transmitter substance involved in memory, ________________ disturbances, and motor coordination. (61)

weight/thickness
transmitter
glial/bodies
occipital
50
synaptic

36. Rats that lived in an enriched environment showed greater ________________ and ________________ of the cerebral cortex, greater total activity of certain ________________ substances, more ________________ cells, and larger cell ________________ and nuclei. The greatest difference was found in the ________________ lobe, which is primarily related to vision. The enriched rats in one study showed a ________________ percent increase in the size of the ________________ junctions in the brain. (59)

PSYCHOLOGICAL ISSUE: *BIOLOGICAL RHYTHMS*

circadian
temperature
hormones
dawn

37. Biological rhythms that take place over a 24-hour period are called ________________ rhythms. These include changes in body ________________, blood pressure, heart rate, blood-sugar level, and secretion of certain ________________. Body temperature is the lowest just before ________________. (65)

morning

38. Our bodies use food most efficiently in the ________________, although

	our senses of smell and taste tend to be most sensitive in the
evening	________________ hours; smell and taste may be related to fluctuations
adrenal	in the level of ________________ hormones. (65)
	39. Short cycles of biological activity, such as heartbeats and breathing, are
ultradian	called ________________ rhythms. Both dream cycles and daytime
90	rest-and-activity seem to follow a ________ -minute cycle. (67)
infradian	**40.** Cycles that take longer than a day are called ________________
	rhythms, and are illustrated by the menstrual cycle, which is about
28	________________ days. Although men show fluctuations in
	testosterone levels, these fluctuations do not correspond to
mood	________________ changes. (67)
	41. Examinations of psychotic episodes and suicides have not shown any
lunar	relationship to the ________________ phase. (68)
suicide	**42.** In North America, ________________ rates and mental hospital
	admissions are at their peak in late spring and early summer. Deaths are
winter	most likely to occur in the ________________. Americans tend to be
happiest	________________ in the spring and summer. Changes in happiness
	may be related to increased day length and likelihood of
sunshine	________________. Solar radiation can indirectly increase the level of
serotonin	the chemical transmitter ________________, in addition to brightening
aesthetic	our mood for ________________ and symbolic reasons. (69)

Self-Quiz

1. As electricity passes through a neuron, which part is out of order?
a. Myelin sheath.
b. Dendrites.
c. Cell body.
d. Axon.

2. Which statement is not true of biological rhythms?
a. The suicide rate is highest in winter.
b. The death rate is highest in winter.
c. Americans tend to be happiest in the spring and summer.
d. Dreams and daytime rest-and-activity patterns seem to follow a 90-minute cycle.

3. Which one of the following statements is false?
a. The central nervous system contains nerves in the arms and legs.
b. The nerves in the brain do not regenerate.
c. The autonomic nervous system is a subdivision of the peripheral nervous system.
d. The sympathetic nervous system is a subdivision of the autonomic nervous system.

4. The human brain is not characterized by which one of the following?
a. It weighs three pounds.
b. It is the largest of all brains in relative size.
c. It contains 110 million neurons and glia.
d. The cerebral cortex is 80 percent of the brain.

5. Which one of the following statements is false?
   a. Efferent neurons are incoming sensory neurons.
   b. The somatic nervous system activates voluntary muscles.
   c. Sympathetic nerves are active when you are feeling stress.
   d. Parasympathetic nerves do the opposite of what sympathetic nerves do.

6. The hypothalamus monitors all but which one of the following?
   a. Eating.
   b. Emotional behavior.
   c. Memories.
   d. Sexual activity.

7. Which statement is not true of the cerebral lobes?
   a. The frontal lobe is believed to be involved in emotional expression.
   b. The parietal lobe keeps us physically oriented in our environment.
   c. The occipital lobe contains the speech center.
   d. The temporal lobe processes auditory information.

8. Which statement is not true of brain waves?
   a. People showing alpha waves report feeling relaxed.
   b. People showing beta waves report feeling fear or worry.
   c. People showing theta waves report feeling anger or excitement.
   d. People showing delta waves are either infants or in deep sleep.

9. The environment has all but which one of the following effects?
   a. Malnutrition causes a reduction of cells in the portion of the brain responsible for motor coordination.
   b. Undernourished children show retardation in both physical and intellectual skills.
   c. Rats in an enriched environment showed greater cortical weight and thickness.
   d. Rats in a visually stimulating environment showed especially noticeable changes in the frontal lobe.

10. Which statement is not representative of the brain's hemispheres?
   a. A hemisphere controls the side of the body the hemisphere is on.
   b. In right-handed people the right hemisphere controls spatial relationships.
   c. The corpus callosum transfers information from one hemisphere to the other.
   d. Epileptics have been successfully treated by cutting the corpus callosum.

Answers: 1.a 2.a 3.a 4.c 5.a 6.c 7.c 8.c 9.d 10.a

Chapter 3

Perception

1. Define perception. Trace the events involved in converting physical energy from the environment into experience. (72)

VISION

2. Locate and describe each of the following: (73)

Cornea—

Pupil—

Iris—

Lens—

Retina—

3. Distinguish between rods and cones in terms of number, structure, location, and function. Define optic nerve and fovea. (74)

4. Describe the process of dark adaptation. Define visual threshold. Distinguish between dark adaptation in rods and in cones. (75)

5. Define: (75)

Visual acuity—

Blind spot—

Nearsightedness—

Farsightedness—

6. What is believed to be the mechanism of color vision? List the colors corresponding to the three types of cones. (76)

7. How prevalent is color blindness, and why are men more likely to be color-blind? Describe three types of color blindness. Which is most common? (76)

8. How is binocular vision involved in depth perception? (77)

9. Define monocular cues. List four of them. (77)

10. Describe the visual cliff experiments. What conclusions can be drawn from the results? (77)

HEARING

11. Describe and locate each of the following: (79)

Tympanic membrane—

Maleus, incus, stapes—

Cochlea—

Auditory nerve—

12. Describe the following in terms of psychological experience and the physical qualities of sound that determine the experience: (79)

Loudness—

Pitch—

Timbre—

13. *BOX 1:* List two harmful effects of noise. What did Glass and Singer conclude about the predictability and controllability of noise? (80)

14. *BOX 1:* Summarize the results of the studies done on noise in city apartment buildings and at a school near an airport. (81)

15. List two factors that enable us to locate the source of a sound. (79)

THE SKIN SENSES

16. What is the sense of touch comprised of? How does pressure sensitivity vary over different parts of the body? (80)

17. To what do hot and cold receptors respond? How are they distributed over the body? (81)

18. What is known and what is still debated about the sense of pain? (83)

19. Describe the specificity theory of pain. What is the major problem with it? (84)

20. Describe Melzack and Wall's theory of pain. Define gate-control mechanisms. (84)

21. *BOX 2:* Define enkephalins and endorphins. Describe their possible roles in acupuncture and the effects of placebos. (83)

22. *BOX 2:* Describe the use of the following to control pain: (83)

Electrical stimulation—

Hypnosis—

Drugs—

KINESTHESIS AND EQUILIBRIUM

23. Describe kinesthesis and how it works. (84)

24. Describe the sense of equilibrium (balance) and how it works. (85)

SMELL AND TASTE

25. Describe the sense of smell and how it works. (85)

26. Describe the sense of taste and how it works. (86)

PERCEPTION AS AN ACTIVE PROCESS

27. What does it mean to say that perception is an active process? (87)

28. *BOX 3:* Summarize the method, results, and conclusions of Heron's study. What are Suedfeld's conclusions about sensory deprivation? (88)

29. Define Gestalt psychology and these three principles of perceptual organization: figure-ground, proximity, and similarity. (87)

30. Define the concept of attention, explaining the role of contrast and novelty. (90)

31. Describe the process of focusing attention and the conclusions from Treisman's experiment. What becomes of material that is filtered out? (91)

32. Define perceptual set. How is it affected by motivation? How does Bruner interpret perceptual set? (91)

33. Define size constancy. What evidence shows it depends on experience to some extent? (93)

34. Define perceptual constancy. Describe color constancy and brightness constancy. How does brightness constancy work? (94)

35. Define perceptual illusion. How do normal correction processes such as size constancy account for illusions? (94)

36. Describe each of the following illusions: (94)

Müller-Lyer—

Ponzo—

Necker cube—

PSYCHOLOGICAL ISSUE: *EXTRASENSORY PERCEPTION*

37. Define ESP and distinguish among clairvoyance, telepathy, and precognition. (99)

38. What is the general procedure in ESP research? List three problems with research on ESP. (99)

39. Summarize the attitudes of psychologists about ESP. What factors underlie these attitudes? (100)

Self-Quiz

1. The receptor cells that are sensitive to light are located in what part of the eye?
   a. Cornea.
   b. Retina.
   c. Iris.
   d. Pupil. (Study Question 2)

2. Visual thresholds and dark adaptation levels are determined by:
   a. genetic predispositions.
   b. the blind spot.
   c. chemical processes.
   d. the brain. (Study Question 4)

3. The three types of cone cells are:
   a. red, yellow, and blue.
   b. red, green, and visual purple.
   c. red, green, and blue.
   d. yellow, blue, and rhodopsin. (Study Question 6)

4. The visual-cliff experiment is used to demonstrate that:
   a. depth perception is innate.
   b. most people do not have 20/20 vision.
   c. infants can perceive checker-board patterns.
   d. a prerequisite to perception is learning and experience. (Study Question 10)

5. The receptor cells for sound are in the:
   a. fovea.
   b. tympanic membrane.
   c. retina.
   d. cochlea. (Study Question 11)

6. The experience of hot on the skin is the result of the excitation of:
   a. warm receptors.
   b. cold receptors.

c. pain receptors.
d. both a and b above. (Study Question 17)

7. The specific receptor for balance is the:
a. olfactory epithelium.
b. tympanic membrane.
c. pacinian corpuscle.
d. semicircular canals. (Study Question 24)

8. The taste receptors in the tongue respond to which of the following tastes?
a. Fruity, sour, burnt, spicy.
b. Burnt, spicy, fruity, resinous.
c. Salt, sweet, fruity, burnt.
d. Salt, sweet, sour, bitter. (Study Question 26)

9. The tendency for a Pygmy who is raised in bush country with no exposure to wide-open spaces to perceive cows from a distance as insects, is an example of an inadequately developed sense of:
a. color constancy.
b. size constancy.
c. form constancy.
d. brightness constancy. (Study Question 33)

10. The illusion shown is known as:
a. Necker illusion.
b. Ponzo illusion.
c. Müller-Lyer illusion.
d. Ames illusion. (Study Question 36)

Answers to Self-Quiz: 1.b 2.c 3.c 4.a 5.d 6.d 7.d 8.d 9.b 10.b

Programmed Review Unit

physical
electrical

1. Sense organs transform the ________ energy (such as light, sound waves, heat) emanating from objects into ________ impulses. (72)

30
20
teaspoon
three

2. A comparison of the sensitivity of your various senses shows you can see a candle flame ________ miles away on a dark night, hear the tick of a watch under quiet conditions at ________ feet, taste one ________ of sugar in two gallons of water, and smell one drop of perfume diffused into a ________ -room apartment. (75)

VISION

cornea
pupil

3. Light first passes through the ________, a transparent protective coating over the front part of the eye, then passes through the ________, an opening that can be enlarged or reduced to let more or less light in by contractions in the muscles of the

Answers	
iris	__________________, the colored part of the eye. Light then passes
lens	through the__________________, which can be adjusted to focus the light
retina	from objects onto the back of the eyeball, the__________________, which
	is analogous to the film in a camera. (73)
6/100	**4.** More than __________________ million cones and __________________
	million rods make up the receptor cells in the retina. The
rods	__________________ are not sensitive to color and are mainly at the edges
fovea	of the retina. The cones are primarily located in the__________________,
	a spot in the retina that is directly behind the lens. The greater the
	amount of rhodopsin in the rods and other light-sensitive chemicals in
threshold	the cones, the lower the visual __________________. Rods are
more	__________________ sensitive to light than cones, and take more than
30	__________________ minutes to completely adapt to darkness. Thus, if
away from	you want to see a dim light in pitch darkness, look __________________
	the object. (74)
	5. The blind spot is the point in each retina at which the nerves converge to
optic nerve	form the __________________. (75)
	6. We have three types of cones, sensitive to the colors of
red/green/blue	__________________, __________________, and __________________.
7	About __________________ percent of the people in the world cannot see
	one or more colors. Most of these partially color-blind people are
men/inherited	__________________, since color blindness is an __________________,
	sex-linked characteristic. The person with yellow-blue blindness sees a
red/green	world of __________________ and __________________; this is the
less	__________________ common of the two types of dichromatic color
	blindness. (76)
size	**7.** Monocular cues such as overlap, relative __________________,
shadow	perspective, and __________________ work even when we use only one
	eye. (77)
	8. Studies with the visual cliff have provided convincing evidence that much
innate	of depth perception is __________________. (77)

HEARING

Answers	
	9. Movements of air molecules called sound waves set into motion a series of
mechanical	__________________ processes in the outer, middle, and inner ear. When
eardrum	sound waves hit the tympanic membrane (the__________________), they
three	move __________________ bones in the middle ear, which sends vibra-
cochlea	tions through fluid in the inner ear, snail-like__________________. (79)
pitch	**10.** The high or low quality of a sound is called its__________________, and is
frequency	determined by the__________________ of wave vibrations. The fact that a
	note played on a violin will not sound exactly like the same note played on
timbre	a trumpet illustrates a difference in __________________. (79)
	11. The Environmental Protection Agency estimates that more than
16	__________________ million people in the U. S. suffer from hearing loss
	caused by noise. At around the middle of the decibel scale, every increase
doubling	in 10 decibels represents an approximate __________________ of sound
	intensity. Children closer to freeway noise in one study had poorer
reading	__________________ skills than children further away from noise. In an-
	other study, children who lived in a noisy area were more likely to fail or
cognitive	a __________________ task (a puzzle) or give up before they needed to. (80)

THE SKIN SENSES

pressure/pain/temperature
six
trunk
hot

12. The sense of touch is actually a combination of at least three sensations: ________, ________, and ________. There are about ________ times as many cold receptors as warm ones in the skin. These temperature receptors are more concentrated along the ________ of the body, which is why the hands and feet can withstand greater temperature extremes. A really ________ stimulus excites both cold and heat receptors. (80)

pain
tissue
reticular formation
brain

13. Very bright lights, loud noises, high or low temperatures, or great pressure all produce ________ sensations, which warn us of ________ destruction. Acupuncture needles are inserted at sites that activate the ________ ________ in the brain stem, one of the gate-control areas of the nervous system, so that pain signals are blocked before they reach the ________. (84)

electrical/hypnosis
placebos

14. In addition to acupuncture, other modern pain control strategies include ________ stimulation, use of ________ in childbirth and dentistry, drugs, and ________, which help the person because she or he believes it will help. (83)

KINESTHESIS AND EQUILIBRIUM

positions
joints
balance or equilibrium
ear
planes
head

15. The sense that tells you the ________ and movements of your muscles and ________ is called kinesthesis. Our sense of ________ works in conjunction with kinesthesis and has its sense organs in the inner ________. The semicircular canals lie on different ________ and are filled with a fluid that moves when you move your ________. (84)

SMELL AND TASTE

gaseous
heavier

16. Most of what we smell comes from ________ chemical molecules that are ________ than air, so that when you stand erect, your nose misses most smells. (85)

sweet/sour
bitter/salty

17. The four basic tastes are ________, ________, ________ and ________. (86)

PERCEPTION AS AN ACTIVE PROCESS

intellectual
persuasible
hallucinations
reticular activating
brain
changing
rare

18. In one sensory deprivation study, after a few days subjects' performance on a variety of ________ tasks was markedly impaired. The subjects also were highly ________, and reported experiencing ________. It appears that, when we are deprived of sensory stimulation, the ________ system slows down, which disturbs the functioning of the ________. This caused Heron to conclude, "A ________ sensory environment seems essential to human beings." On the other hand, Suedfeld (1975) found that sensory deprivation does not necessarily harm intellectual functioning and sometimes even improves it. This study found that severe emotional reactions to sensory deprivation are extremely ________. One of the reasons that negative reactions have been reported may be that the

expectations
visual
auditory

subjects were swayed by their ________. In some cases, sensory deprivation may sharpen the subjects' ________ and ________ acuity. (89)

whole
proximity
similarity

19. Gestalt psychologists emphasized our perception of figures and forms as a ________. We tend to organize our perceptions of elements in terms of their ________ and ________ to each other. (87)

attention/contrast
novelty
physical
meaning

20. The process of focusing on some stimuli while ignoring others is called ________. Berlyne (1970) found that ________ and ________ are characteristics that consistently grab attention. We are able to keep track of one conversation and ignore others by relying on ________ cues such as the sound pattern of particular voices and the direction they are coming from. We are also able to separate messages according to their ________. (90)

expect
Motivation

21. We demonstrate perceptual set when we perceive what we ________, while remaining unaware of other things. ________ can also affect perceptual set, so we tend to focus on things that we consider important. (91)

doubles
size

22. If a person moves from 20 feet away to 10 feet away, the height of the image on your retina ________. Fortunately, ________ constancy develops quickly as a result of experience. (93)

illusions

23. Instances in which perception and reality do not agree are called ________. (94)

PSYCHOLOGICAL ISSUE: *EXTRASENSORY PERCEPTION*

clairvoyance
telepathy
precognition
science

24. The use of extrasensory perception to know about an object or event is called ________, while being aware of another's thoughts without communicating through normal sensory channels is called ________. Foreknowledge of future events is called ________. ESP has yet to be demonstrated conclusively according to the rules of established ________. (99)

Self-Quiz

1. If you have 20/20 vision and your friend has 20/50 vision:
- **a.** you see distant things better than he does.
- **b.** he sees distant things better than you do.
- **c.** you both see distant things equally well.
- **d.** you both need glasses.

2. Which statement is false?
- **a.** You can see a candle flame 30 miles away.
- **b.** Much of what we know about the outside world comes through our eyes.
- **c.** The E.P.A. estimates that more than 16 million Americans suffer from environmentally-induced hearing loss.
- **d.** Trumpets and violins playing the same note display different pitch.

3. Which statement is not true of the functions of the retina?
- **a.** There are 6 million cones and 100 million rods in each retina.

b. The rods are color-blind and are more sensitive to light.
c. The rods are primarily located in the fovea.
d. If you want to see a dim light at night look slightly away from it.

4. Which one of the following statements is false?
a. Instances in which perception and reality do not agree are called illusions.
b. Perceptual set occurs when we do not perceive what we do not expect.
c. Noise reduces children's demonstrated reading skills.
d. Acupuncture works by focusing your attention on a new source of pain.

5. Which one of the following statements is not true of colorblindness?
a. It is more common in men.
b. There are three types of colorblindness.
c. About 7 percent of the world's people are colorblind.
d. Yellow-blue colorblindness is the most common type of dichromatic colorblindness.

6. Which one of the following statements is not true of the sense of touch?
a. Touch is a combination of pressure, pain, and temperature.
b. There are six times as many hot receptors as cold receptors.
c. Temperature receptors are concentrated on the trunk of the body.
d. A very hot stimulus excites both hot and cold receptors.

7. Which one of the following statements is not true of the senses?
a. You have sensors which tell you the positions of your joints.
b. You have sensors which tell you the movements of your muscles.
c. Your sense of balance works in conjunction with your sense of kinesthesis.
d. Your organs for your sense of balance are located in your joints.

8. Which one of the following statements is not true of ESP?
a. Clairvoyance is communication through other than normal sensory channels.
b. Psychokinesis is influencing an object through will power.
c. Precognition is foreknowledge of future events.
d. Most American psychologists are doubtful about the existence of ESP.

9. Which one of the following statements is false?
a. Acupuncture needles cause the reticular activating system to keep pain from reaching the brain.
b. Steak has almost no taste.
c. Our perceptions can be distorted by what we expect or value.
d. We have eight different taste receptors.

10. If the driver of a Saab hears 70 decibels and the driver of a Pinto hears 80 db, how much louder is the Pinto?
a. One-seventh louder.
b. Twice as loud.
c. Four times as loud.
d. Both cars are above the pain threshold.

Answers: 1.b 2.d 3.c 4.d 5.d 6.b 7.d 8.a 9.d 10.b

Chapter 4

Consciousness

THE NATURE OF CONSCIOUSNESS

1. Define consciousness. Give two ways in which the term unconscious is used. (102)

2. How does consciousness vary in quality and perceptual accuracy? (103)

3. Describe the early study of consciousness and its recent revival. Explain dualism. (104)

4. *BOX 1:* Describe three types of daydreamers. How are daydreams related to gender, age, and night dreams? (106)

5. *BOX 1:* Summarize Singer's speculations about why we daydream. (106)

SLEEP

6. Discuss the problem of why we must sleep. What is the average amount of sleep and how does it vary with age and from day to day? (105)

7. Describe falling asleep and the effects of sleep deprivation. (108)

8. *BOX 2:* Summarize the behavioral and psychological differences between long-sleepers and short-sleepers. How does Hartmann's theory account for these differences? (111)

9. Describe the following stages of sleep: (109)

Stage 1—

Stage 2—

Stage 3—

Stage 4—

10. Describe REM sleep. How does the sleeper progress through the stages of sleep? (109)

11. Define non-REM sleep. What are the differences between REM and non-REM sleep? Define paradoxical sleep. (110)

12. Describe insomnia and its causes. How is it affected by sleeping pills and alcohol? (112)

13. Define: (113)

Narcolepsy—

Sleepwalking—

Night terrors—

DREAMING

14. Describe the Freudian interpretation of dreams and the concepts of symbolism, condensation, and displacement. (114)

15. Distinguish between the latent and manifest content of dreams. How has Freud's approach been criticized? (114)

16. Describe the activation-synthesis model of dreams. (115)

17. What are the effects of REM deprivation? (116)

18. According to Freud and Jung, why do we need to dream? Summarize Cartwright's research. Can dreams be controlled? (110)

DRUGS

19. Define psychoactive drugs. How do their effects come about? (117)

20. *BOX 3:* Describe the effects of: (124)

Nicotine—

Caffeine—

Ethyl alcohol—

21. List six reasons for drug use. How do the drug use patterns of students compare with their parents? (118)

22. Describe LSD, its effects, and how it works. List three original uses of LSD, and two other substances with similar effects. (118)

23. Summarize the history of marijuana, its current use, and its physiological effects. (119)

24. List the general conclusions about the effects of marijuana on behavior. What are its medically beneficial effects? (120)

25. Summarize the history of amphetamines and their current use. (121)

26. Describe the effects of a continuous amphetamine high, including amphetamine psychosis. How do amphetamines produce their effects? (121)

27. Summarize the history of cocaine, its effects on behavior and physiology, and its current use. (123)

HYPNOSIS

28. Define: (124)

Hypnosis—

Hypnotic amnesia—

Posthypnotic suggestion—

29. Describe the Stanford Hypnotic Susceptibility Scale. How does susceptibility vary by gender and age? (125)

30. What kinds of pain have been relieved by hypnosis? Describe Hilgard's concept of dissociation. (126)

31. What does Barber believe about hypnosis? Describe Orne's research. (127)

PSYCHOLOGICAL ISSUE: *MEDITATION*

32. Summarize the process of meditation. Describe two kinds of meditation, their different physiological effects, and how attention is regulated. Is meditation related to alpha production? (131)

33. Define relaxation response and list its four necessary elements. (133)

34. Describe the physiological effects of transcendental meditation found by Wallace and Benson and others. How is TM related to drug use? (133)

Self-Quiz

1. Consciousness:
   a. is central to our routine activities.
   b. always enhances the behavior it is focused on.
   c. is obvious when we are learning a new skill.
   d. is essential for all behaviors. (Study Question 1)

2. The current strategy for studying consciousness:
   a. is to concentrate on normal consciousness.
   b. is to rely more heavily on introspection.
   c. is connected to the revolution in brain research.
   d. all of the above. (Study Question 3)

3. Which statement is true about sleep?
   a. In some parts of the world people get along with less than 4 hours of sleep.
   b. If you are a college student, 8 hours of sleep is the right amount for you.
   c. In middle and old age people sleep more.
   d. It is still a mystery why sleep is necessary for survival. (Study Question 6)

4. According to Hartmann, long-sleepers are characterized by which of the following?
   a. Extroverted, carefree, and confident behavior.
   b. More creative behavior.
   c. More productive behavior.
   d. More efficient and practical behavior. (Study Question 8)

5. From experiments in which people were awakened during different stages of sleep, we can conclude that most dreaming occurs during:
   a. all stages of non-REM sleep.
   b. paradoxical sleep.
   c. Stages 2 and 3 of sleep.
   d. Stage 4 of sleep. (Study Question 11)

6. According to Freud:
   a. dreams serve to point out one's weaknesses.
   b. dreams consist of wish-fulfilling symbols.
   c. the dream that we recall in the morning is the latest dream.
   d. dreams serve no particular purpose unless they are analyzed. (Study Question 14)

7. According to the activation-synthesis model, what may cause the bizarre content of our dreams?
   a. Unusually intense and rapid brain activity in unrelated areas.
   b. Unconscious wishes.
   c. Rapid firing of the reticular activating system arousing the limbic system.
   d. Latent aggression and hostility. (Study Question 16)

8. The effects of LSD depend to a great extent on:
   a. the personal characteristics of the user.
   b. the setting in which the drug is taken.
   c. the purity of the substance.
   d. all of the above. (Study Question 22)

9. Amphetamine psychosis is characterized by:
   a. paranoid delusions.
   b. nonsensical speech patterns.
   c. inappropriate facial expressions.
   d. attacks of amnesia. (Study Question 26)

10. Which of the following is not found for experienced meditators?
    a. Lower blood pressure.
    b. Slower reaction time.
    c. Decreased anxiety.
    d. Increased emotional stability. (Study Question 34)

Answers to Self-Quiz: 1.c 2.c 3.d 4.b 5.b 6.b 7.a 8.d 9.a 10.b

Programmed Review Unit

subjective

1. Consciousness refers to our ________________ awareness of our own actions and the world around us. (102)

THE NATURE OF CONSCIOUSNESS

unconscious
aggressive
threatening

2. Although consciousness is not essential for all behaviors, it may be applied to normally ________________ acts like walking. Freud had a different meaning for unconscious, believing that part of the mind to contain sexual and ________________ impulses that were too ________________ to think about consciously. (103)

introspection
unreliable
overt
dualism

3. The structuralists sought to learn about consciousness through ________________ —the careful examination of their own conscious experience. The introspective method was often ________________ and gave way to behaviorism, which focused on ________________ behavior. The idea that the mind is separated from the brain is called ________________. (104)

failure
criticism or doubt
hostile
positive
visual/acceptance
less
related
90
intellectual
control

4. There appear to be three types of daydreamers: the first type has rather anxious daydreams, often centered on fears of ________________; the second type focuses on self-________________ and is most likely to have ________________ fantasies; the third type has ________________ fantasies that usually include clear ________________ images and reflect self-________________. People seem to daydream ________________ as they get older. Our daydreams and night dreams are probably ________________ to each other, as evidenced by the fact that both seem to peak every ________________ minutes. Daydreams may promote optimal ________________ functioning, self-________________, and a peaceful inner life.

rewards

Daydreaming also can provide us with ________ we need when the world around us fails to do so. (107)

SLEEP

7.4
less
REM
2
norepinephrine

5. The average college student sleeps ________ hours a night (8.5 hours on weekends). As you get older you tend to sleep ________ each night. The length of time you sleep seems to be related to the amount of ________ sleep you have; long sleepers spend almost ________ hours each night in this type of sleep compared to only 1 hour for short sleepers. REM sleep may help to restore the effectiveness of the brain transmitter substance called ________. (106)

falling asleep
easy
bursts of activity
long/slow
deepest
15/30
first
lessens

6. Stage 1 is ________; in Stage 1 the person is ________ to awaken. In Stage 2, brain waves show ________ called spindles. In Stage 3 the brain waves become ________ and ________ (about one wave per second). Stage 4 is the ________ sleep, called delta sleep, and in young adults occurs in ________ or ________ minute segments during the ________ half of the night. Delta sleep ________ with age. (109)

rapid eye movement/dream
paradoxical
faster/higher

7. In Stages 1 through 4 a person will not show REMs, or ________. During REM sleep, we ________. REM periods get longer as the night goes on. REM sleep is often referred to as ________ sleep because the brain seems to be highly activated even though the person is asleep. During REM sleep pulse and respiration are a bit ________ and blood pressure is ________ than in non-REM sleep. (110)

40
older/sleeping pills
alcohol
sleep attacks
children
4
deep
3/5

8. In one study, over ________ percent of adults have had problems staying asleep; insomnia is most prevalent among ________ people. Paradoxically, both ________ and ________ can produce insomnia. If a person has narcolepsy, he is a victim of ________. Sleepwalking is most common among ________, and appears to be done during Stage ________ sleep. Night terrors, unlike nightmares, wake a person from ________ sleep; these are most common between the ages of ________ and ________. (112)

DREAMING

unconscious
tension
symbolism
condensation
displacement

9. Freud believed that ________ impulses are responsible for dreams, which reduce the ________ created by these impulses. He thought dreams function to preserve sleep by disguising these impulses through the use of ________ (their presentation in a more acceptable form), ________ (the representation of several elements in one image), and ________ (the focusing of an unacceptable wish on an object different from the real object). (114)

10. The recent activation-synthesis model of dreaming states that dreams

nerve cells brain stem brain	begin with the periodic firing of ________ located in the ________. We synthesize a dream mentally, coming up with content that corresponds to the pattern of ________ activation. (115)
2 more concentrating/ hallucinate	**11.** Young adults dream about ________ hours a night on the average. Dement (1960) found that people who were deprived of REM sleep had ________ REM sleep the next few nights. REM-deprived people also are more anxious and irritable, have difficulty ________, and are more likely to ________. (116)
balance	**12.** Jung felt that dreams serve to restore our overall psychological ________. (116)
realistically esteem	**13.** Cartwright (1978) found that people seem to handle emotional situations more ________ after dreaming; she concluded dreams repaired self- ________ and competence. (117)

DRUGS

psychoactive addictive sympathetic blood pressure stimulant/Alcohol	**14.** Chemicals that affect mood, behavior, or perception are called ________ drugs. Caffeine and nicotine are mildly ________. Nicotine blocks transmission in the ________ nervous system, elevates heart rate and ________. Caffeine is a central nervous system ________. ________ abuse is the biggest drug problem in America today. (117)
transmitter	**15.** Psychoactive drugs often interfere with the normal function of the brain's ________ substances. (117)
parents	**16.** Young people may often use their ________ as models in deciding whether or not to try drugs. (118)
Peyote mescaline/color	**17.** ________ (a Mexican cactus) is made up of alkaloids (one of which is ________) that produce intense ________ awareness and hallucinations. (118)
perceptual emotional serotonin emotions	**18.** LSD-25 produces a profound alteration of sensory, ________, cognitive, and ________ experiences. LSD may block the effects of the transmitter substance called ________, which usually acts to inhibit thought processes and ________.
43 10 heart rate/appetite waves permanent addictive perceptual coordination emotionally	**19.** As of 1979, an estimated ________ million Americans had smoked marijuana at least once; a 1978 survey showed that over ________ percent of high-school seniors were daily users. Marijuana has two easily observable physiological effects: it increases ________ and enhances ________. It also changes brain ________, although it probably does not cause ________ brain damage. Although marijuana is not ________, some users need greater amounts to achieve the same effect. Marijuana reduces ________ acuity and ________ and may be risky for the young or the ________ troubled. Marijuana may be useful in treating some physical problems. (119)
amphetamines anxiety/nightmares	**20.** When the high from taking ________ is over, the physical and psychological effects can be quite uncomfortable; the user may experience extreme fatigue, ________, terrifying ________

depression
paranoid
dopamine

severe __________, disorientation, and confusion. Amphetamine psychosis resembles the psychological disorder known as __________ schizophrenia. Amphetamines seem to trigger the release of the neurotransmitter called __________. (121)

stimulant
confidence
talkativeness
irritability/exhaustion
depression
physiological

21. Like amphetamine, cocaine is a __________. Cocaine produces feelings of alertness and self-__________, often accompanied by __________; it may also produce nervousness, __________, restlessness, and __________, as well as mild __________ when "coming down." Cocaine does not appear to cause __________ dependence. (123)

HYPNOSIS

suggestibility
8 to 10
physiological
sensory
emotional

22. Hypnosis is a state of increased __________. Susceptibility to hypnosis rises in childhood, peaks at ages __________, then declines slowly after that. When given the suggestion that they will feel no pain, hypnotized people feel little pain, their __________ responses may reflect the sensation of pain. Hilgard (1977) thus concludes that pain has two components: the __________ aspect and the __________ aspect, which can be dissociated. (125)

EEG

23. Barber (1970) points out that hypnotized subjects do not exhibit an __________ pattern different from nonhypnotized subjects; his research suggests that anything you can do while hypnotized you can do in a wide-awake state. (127)

PSYCHOLOGICAL ISSUE: *MEDITATION*

passivity
experience
do
relax
distractions
object
physiological
external
consistent or persistent
regulation

24. Meditation leads to a deep __________ combined with awareness—a suspension of the usual rat race of mental and physical activity in order to __________ things rather than just __________ them. The position used in meditation should let you __________ without letting you fall asleep. In meditation you practice concentrating and eliminating __________ by bringing your attention back again to the __________ of your meditation every time it wanders. The two approaches to meditation appear to result in different __________ effects. The type that involves restriction of awareness results in reduced responsiveness to __________ stimuli, such as loud noises. In the opening-up type of meditation practitioners show a __________ response to external stimuli. Both forms place a critical emphasis on self-__________ of attention. (131)

detachment
pleasant

25. People who were high-responders to meditation in one study described the state as one of extreme __________ from the outside world, and having __________ bodily sensations. (132)

alpha

26. People showing the __________ rhythm brain wave pattern report being relaxed. (132)

environment
muscle/passive

27. Benson suggests that four elements are necessary to elicit the relaxation response: (a) a quiet __________, (b) decreased __________ tone, (c) a __________ attitude, and (d) a

thought	mental device so that attention can be shifted from logical ________________ to an object or sound. (133)
oxygen/heartbeat **respiration/brain waves** **cardiovascular/reaction** **anxiety** **assurance/stability** **drugs**	**28.** Wallace and Benson (1972) found that meditators consumed less ________________, slowed their ________________ and ________________, and altered their ________________. Other investigators found that experienced meditators showed improved ________________ efficiency, faster ________________ times, lower blood pressure, decreased ________________, and increased self-________________ and emotional ________________. Meditation also appears to reduce interest in ________________. (133)

Self-Quiz

1. Which one of the following statements is not true of nicotine?
a. It blocks transmission in the sympathetic nervous system.
b. It blocks transmission in the autonomic nervous system.
c. It elevates blood pressure.
d. It dilates peripheral blood vessels.

2. Which one of the following statements is not true of the studies of meditation?
a. It appears to increase interest in drugs.
b. Meditators feel more relaxed.
c. Meditators experience pleasant bodily sensations.
d. Meditators consume less oxygen.

3. Which statement is not true of daydreaming?
a. There are five types of daydreams.
b. One type focuses on failure.
c. One type reflects self-acceptance.
d. Daydreams promote intellectual functioning.

4. Stage 4 sleep is characterized by all but which one of the following?
a. It is the deepest sleep.
b. It lessens with age.
c. It occurs primarily in the first half of the night.
d. In young adults it occurs in 60 to 90 minute intervals.

5. Which one of the following statements is not true of REM sleep?
a. Longer sleepers have more REM sleep.
b. It does not occur in Stages 1 through 4.
c. People spend from 3 to 4 hours a night in REM sleep.
d. People dream in REM sleep.

6. Which one of the following statements is not true of dreaming?
a. Blood pressure drops when one dreams.
b. A minority of people remember a dream they had the night before.
c. There is a need to make up dreaming time that has been lost.
d. Freud thought that dreams reduce tension and keep you asleep.

7. Hypnosis is a state of increased:
a. intensity.
b. sleepiness.
c. suggestibility.
d. unconsciousness.

8. Which one of the following statements is not true?
a. Hypnosis reduced pain in dental patients.
b. Hard thinking will make you sleepy.
c. Marijuana is not physically addicting.
d. Daydreaming can be a way of providing us with rewards.

9. In 1978, what percent of high-school seniors were daily users of marijuana?
a. 5 percent.
b. 1 percent.
c. over 10 percent.
d. 51 percent.

10. Marijuana has all but which one of the following effects?
a. It increases the pulse rate.
b. It increases the appetite.
c. It increases sexual energy.
d. It impairs coordination.

Answers: 1.d 2.a. 3.a 4.d 5.c 6.a 7.c 8.b 9.c 10.c

Chapter 5

Learning

1. Define the following: (137)

   Learning—

   Reflexes—

   Instincts—

   Inherited capacities—

CLASSICAL CONDITIONING

2. Define conditioning and distinguish between classical and operant conditioning. (138)

3. Define: (138)

   Unconditioned stimulus—

   Unconditioned response—

   Neutral stimulus—

Conditioned stimulus—

Conditioned response—

4. Using the terms above, outline the steps in classical conditioning: before, during, and after conditioning. (139)

5. Using the terms from Question 3, describe the examples of Bob and Fred and advertising a product. Create examples of your own until you are thoroughly familiar with the terminology and procedures of classical conditioning. (139)

6. Describe the Staats' demonstration of conditioning. Define semantic conditioning. How does it explain irrational attitudes? (140)

7. Explain the processes of extinction and spontaneous recovery. (141)

8. Explain the processes of generalization and discrimination. Give examples of each from Pavlov's experiments. (142)

OPERANT CONDITIONING

9. Define operant conditioning and its central principle. Describe a Skinner box. (143)

10. *BOX 1:* What is Skinner's conception of superstitious behavior? (142)

11. Define: (144)

Behavior shaping—

Successive approximations—

Behavior modification—

12. Explain the processes of extinction, generalization, and discrimination in operant conditioning. Define discriminative stimulus and stimulus control. (145)

13. Define reinforcement and distinguish between primary and secondary reinforcers. (146)

14. Define and distinguish positive and negative reinforcement. What is the effect of delay of reinforcement? (147)

15. *BOX 2:* Describe biofeedback, the procedures involved, and the responses it has been used to modify. (148)

16. *BOX 2:* How do subjects say they regulate internal responses? What factors make operant conditioning of these responses most effective? What have been the results of applying these techniques in treating illnesses? (148)

17. Define extinction. Distinguish continuous and partial reinforcement. When is each most effective? Why? (149)

18. List the defining characteristics of each of the following kinds of reinforcement schedules: (151)

Ratio—

Interval—

Fixed—

Variable—

19. Define, distinguish among, and give examples of each of the four basic schedules of reinforcement. (151)

20. Compare the reinforcement schedules in terms of their effects on behavior. Define mixed schedules. (152)

21. Define punishment. How does it differ from negative reinforcement? (152)

22. How does punishment work? What is the basic problem with punishment? List three other problems. (153)

COGNITIVE LEARNING

23. Explain the differences between the stimulus-response and cognitive approaches to learning. (154)

24. *BOX 3:* Describe Seligman and Darley's experiment. Define feedback and list the reasons for its effectiveness. (155)

25. What is the associationistic view of maze learning? What two kinds of evidence support Tolman's view? Define latent learning. (156)

26. Define cognitive maps. How do they develop in children? (157)

27. How does learning by observation (modeling) point up the distinction between learning and performance? What two things are learned by observation? (158)

PSYCHOLOGICAL ISSUE: *BEHAVIOR CONTROL*

28. Define: (162)

Behavior modification—

Token economy—

29. What is novel about the approach of behavior modifiers? Summarize the arguments of the behaviorists and the humanists. (163)

30. Summarize the issues involved in three criticisms of behavior control. (164)

31. Describe self-modification (self-reinforcement) and how it is applied. (165

Self-Quiz

1. Classical conditioning involves:
   a. operant responses.
   b. skilled responses.
   c. involuntary responses.
   d. voluntary responses. (Study Question 2)

2. If you shine light into a person's eyes it will cause the pupils to contract. Pupil contraction is a (an):
   a. conditioned response.
   b. unconditioned response.
   c. orienting response.
   d. instinctive response. (Study Question 3)

3. If you condition a response to one stimulus while extinguishing the response to a similar stimulus, you are training for:
   a. generalization.
   b. higher-order conditioning.
   c. extinction.
   d. discrimination. (Study Question 8)

4. An example of behavior learned through successive approximation is:
   a. feeling hungry when the lunch bell rings.
   b. stopping the car at a red light.
   c. a baby smiling.
   d. a dog sitting up and begging. (Study Question 11)

5. In operant conditioning, if reinforcement no longer follows the response, the response will undergo:
   a. differentiation.
   b. extinction.
   c. generalization.
   d. shaping. (Study Question 12)

6. Partial reinforcement schedules are more effective in maintaining a response than continuous reinforcement schedules, because:
   a. subjects do not tire easily.
   b. subjects cannot anticipate the number of responses necessary for the reward.
   c. subjects are given part of the reward now, and part later.
   d. all of the above. (Study Question 17)

7. We can decrease the frequency of behavior by:
   a. positive reinforcement of the behavior.
   b. negative reinforcement of the behavior.
   c. punishment of the behavior.
   d. both b and c. (Study Question 21)

8. Information on how well we are doing on a task is called:
   a. feedback.
   b. behavior information processing.
   c. structural analysis.
   d. cognitive information conditioning. (Study Question 24)

9. Learning which occurs through observation in the absence of an external reinforcer is called:
   a. primary behavior.
   b. secondary behavior.
   c. constructive behavior.
   d. modeled behavior. (Study Question 27)

10. According to B. F. Skinner, freedom of choice:
   a. is a prerequisite for human growth.
   b. is compatible with the implications of scientific analysis.
   c. allows us to choose not to be controlled.
   d. is a myth. (Study Question 29)

Answers to Self-Quiz: 1.c 2.b 3.d 4.d 5.b 6.b 7.c 8.a 9.d 10.d

Programmed Review Unit

change / behavior / reflexes / instincts / species/age

1. Learning is defined as a relatively permanent ________ in ________ as the result of experience or practice. Two types of behavior that are not learned are ________ —automatic responses to stimuli—and ________ —complex, inborn, fixed patterns of behavior that are exhibited by all members of ________ (of the appropriate ________ and sex). (136)

CLASSICAL CONDITIONING

stimuli / responses / involuntary / Operant / punishments

2. In both types of conditioning, particular ________ (objects or events in the world) set up the conditions for the occurrence of our ________ (the behaviors we perform). Classical conditioning focuses on the way in which ________ responses may be linked to stimuli. ________ conditioning focuses on the way in which voluntary responses may be linked to the rewards and ________ we receive for making them. (137)

associated / reflex / unconditioned / response / conditioned / conditioned

3. In classical conditioning stimuli that are merely ________ with food produce the same response that food does. Food presented to an animal elicits the response of salivation; this is a ________ that occurs automatically. Pavlov called the food the ________ stimulus and salivation the unconditioned ________. If a bell was associated with food so that the bell elicited salivation, then it is a ________ stimulus, and the same response of salivation is now called a ________ response. (138)

emotional / attitudes

4. In humans, classical conditioning plays an important role in learning ________ responses. The Staats (1958) demonstrated that ________ toward vocational groups can be established

unconditioned
stimulus
extinction
unlearning
reappears

through classical conditioning. For a classically conditioned response to continue, there need to be repeated pairings of the ________________ stimulus and the conditioned ________________. If the pairing does not occur, the response becomes weaker. Such weakening of a learned response is called ________________, and involves active ________________ of the response. In spontaneous recovery, an extinguished response suddenly ________________. (140)

similar
generalization
discriminate

5. Stimuli ________________ to the conditioned stimulus can produce a similar conditioned response; this is called ________________. In contrast, if an animal has learned to ________________, it will respond to one stimulus and extinguish the response to a similar stimulus. (142)

OPERANT CONDITIONING

reinforcement
operates

6. The central principle of operant conditioning is that animals will produce particular behaviors if they learn that those behaviors will be followed by ________________—some event that is rewarding. Thus the person ________________ on the environment in order to get a reward or avoid a punishment. (143)

shaping
similar
progressively
approximation

7. We can teach an animal complex behavior through the process of behavior ________________. This is done by first rewarding any response that is ________________ to the desired response, and then rewarding responses that are ________________ more like the desired response. This is called the method of successive ________________. (144)

superstitious

8. Skinner believes that humans develop ________________ behavior by being accidentally reinforced by a mistakenly associated reward. (142)

behavior
25
extinguished

9. The alteration of behavior through the principles of learning is called ________________ modification. In one study, teachers reinforced children's cross-sex cooperative play, which increased from about 5 percent to ________________ percent of the children's time. In the absence of reinforcement, the new behavior in this study was ________________; in other cases it was continued. (145)

discriminative
stimulus

10. The state of your father's mood serves as a ________________ stimulus in signalling whether he will be receptive to an idea you want to discuss. If you only cross the street when the light is green your behavior is under ________________ control. (146)

increases
primary
secondary

11. A reinforcement is any event following a response that ________________ the likelihood of that response occurring again. Food, water, and affection are called ________________ reinforcers, while secondary reinforcers become reinforcing by association with primary reinforcers. Money is a ________________ reinforcer. (146)

positive
after
removal
positively
stopped

12. In ________________ reinforcement, a rewarding stimulus is presented ________________ the response, which strengthens the response. In negative reinforcement, the response is strengthened by the ________________ or avoidance of an unpleasant stimulus. Students' laughter would ________________ reinforce an instructor's joke-telling behavior, while the students would negatively reinforce the instructor's joke-telling behavior if they ________________ whispering whenever the instructor told a joke. (147)

effective

13. Delayed reinforcement is less ________________ than reinforcement that comes immediately after the desired response. (149)

schedule

14. The frequency or rate at which reinforcement occurs determines the particular ________________ of reinforcement. If your response is

continuous	reinforced every time, you are being given ________________
	reinforcement; however partial reinforcement is more
common/Partial	________________. ________________ reinforcement makes a
	response more resistent to extinction. (149)
	15. Control of "involuntary" behaviors such as one's heartbeat has been
operant	achieved through ________________ conditioning coupled with
	biofeedback. Patients who improved the most were in programs that
relaxation	included ________________ training and biofeedback training. (148)
	16. When you wait for a number of responses to occur before giving each
ratio	reinforcement you are using a ________________ schedule of
	reinforcement. On the other hand, if time must pass before the
interval	reinforcement is given, then an ________________ schedule is being
fixed	used. Ratio and interval schedules may either be ________________ or
variable	________________. If you had a job in which you were paid for every
	twenty products you turned out, you would be working on a
fixed ratio	________________ schedule; slot machines reward gamblers on a
variable ratio	________________ schedule. Jobs with salaries on regular paydays
fixed interval	illustrate a ________________ schedule, while surprise quizzes
variable interval	demonstrate a ________________ schedule. Ratio schedules produce
higher	________________ response rates than those produced by interval
	schedules. (150)
punishment	**17.** If a response is followed by ________________, then the likelihood the
	response will be repeated is decreased. But punished behavior may
reappear	________________ once the punishment is stopped. Also, punishment
should	does not tell people or animals what they ________________ do; that is
alternative	accomplished by rewarding a clearly available ________________
rewards	response. "Punishments" may actually be ________________ that
	strengthen a response in some people. And the punishment may come to
avoided	be associated with the punisher so that person is ________________.
stress or anxiety	And, finally, punishment often gives rise to ________________, which is
	not helpful for efficient learning. Psychologists, therefore, prefer to use
reinforcement	positive or negative ________________ in altering behavior. (152)

COGNITIVE LEARNING

	18. The cognitive approach to learning emphasizes the acquisition and
information	organization of ________________, namely, how people come to
know	________________ about their world. (154)
feedback	**19.** Information about how well one is doing is called ________________
	and is important in learning if one is successful: when people are given
improves	feedback their performance generally ________________. Families in
less	the feedback group used 10.5 percent ________________ energy than
information	families in the control group. Feedback provides ________________ and
	motivation, as well as reinforcement. (154)
reinforcement	**20.** Tolman suggested that ________________ is not necessary for learning;
latent	this is called ________________ learning. Also, Tolman believed that
	rats did not memorize turns in a maze but instead developed a cognitive
map	or mental ________________ of the entire maze. (156)
modeling	**21.** Learning by observation, or ________________, may occur without
performance	being demonstrated by actual ________________, the production of the
	learned response. Bandura (1973) found that if a child observes an adult
aggressive	being rewarded for performing ________________ responses, the child
	is likely to engage in similar behavior when given the opportunity later. (

PSYCHOLOGICAL ISSUE: *BEHAVIOR CONTROL*

Answers	
token 81 6	**22.** The ________ economy relies on the fact that people will often behave in ways they know will lead to future rewards. Littering in a theater declined from ________ percent to ________ percent when patrons were given litter bags and offered a dime for each bag of litter turned in. (162)
external/humanists myth controls	**23.** The behaviorists tend to emphasize control of our behavior by ________ forces, while the ________ emphasize our ability to make choices and judgments on our own. Skinner (1971) believes that free will is a ________, and that our behavior is entirely determined by external forces. On the other hand, we must ask who ________ the controllers? (163)
smiles/eye 400 zero learning control increase rewards punishments	**24.** A group of incorrigible junior-high students were taught to use rewards such as ________, praise, ________ contact, and shows of interest to shape their teachers' behavior toward them. This led to a ________ percent increase in positive teacher-student contacts along with a reduction of negative contacts to ________. The teachers were happy because the students were ________, and the students were happy because they could ________ their relationships with the teachers. Behavior modification may ________ people's freedom by helping to liberate them from continuing habits or behaviors. Proponents of behavior modification tend to use ________ rather than ________. (164)
themselves stimulus reinforcement before	**25.** People can use behavioral techniques to control ________. An overweight person who only passes a candy store after eating a big meal is demonstrating a ________ control technique. Self-________ is shown by a person who rewards himself for doing something; however, the reward should not be given ________ the desired behavior. (165)

Self-Quiz

1. The schedule of reinforcement that produces the lowest rate of response is the ________ schedule.
   - **a.** fixed-interval
   - **b.** variable-interval
   - **c.** fixed-ratio
   - **d.** variable-ratio

2. Which one of the following statements is not true?
   - **a.** Skinner believes that freedom of choice is a prerequisite for human growth.
   - **b.** Rogers has doubts about external behavior control.
   - **c.** Behavior modification can be done to oneself.
   - **d.** Littering declined from 81 percent to 6 percent when people were paid for full litter bags.

3. Which one of the following statements is not true of the study on incorrigible junior-high students?

a. They were taught to use smiles, eye contact, praise, and displays of interest.
b. Positive teacher-student contacts increased 200 percent.
c. Negative contacts were reduced to zero.
d. Both the teachers and students were happy with the results.

4. Initially, our reinforcements are:
a. physical.
b. social.
c. cognitive.
d. emotional.

5. Instinctive behaviors show which one of the following characteristics?
a. They are learned.
b. They are reflexes.
c. They appear in all members of the species of appropriate age and sex.
d. They appear in humans.

6. Which one of the following statements is not true of cognitive learning?
a. Feedback improves performance.
b. Learning is the same as performance.
c. Children learn aggressive behavior by observing aggressive adults.
d. Tolman believed rats developed cognitive maps which helped them run mazes.

7. Paying a bill to avoid the return of a bill collector demonstrates:
a. positive reinforcement.
b. negative reinforcement.
c. punishment.
d. classical conditioning.

8. If a child is to learn a desired behavior, positively reinforce him:
a. just before the desired behavior.
b. at the time he does the desired behavior.
c. just after the desired behavior.
d. at the end of the day.

9. Punishment is characterized by all but which one of the following?
a. Responses established by punishment are resistant to punishment.
b. Responses may not be eliminated by punishment.
c. Punishment may be a reward.
d. Psychologists prefer punishment to negative reinforcement.

10. If you are being paid a monthly salary, you are being reinforced on what schedule?
a. Fixed-interval.
b. Variable-interval.
c. Fixed-ratio.
d. Variable-ratio.

Answers: 1.a 2.a 3.b 4.a 5.c 6.b 7.b 8.c 9.d 10.a

Chapter 6

Memory

SHORT-TERM AND LONG-TERM MEMORY

1. Distinguish two types of memory noted by William James. Describe sensory storage. (167)

2. What is the capacity of short-term memory, and how can it be expanded? What other limits are there on short-term memory? What happens to information that is not lost in short-term memory? (169)

3. Define long-term memory and describe the processes of rehearsal and encoding. (171)

4. Describe clustering in the recall of lists. What does this phenomenon illustrate? (171)

5. Describe the Hyde and Jenkins experiment. What exceptions are there to the need for encoding? (171)

6. Describe retrieved problems and two ways to improve information retrieval. (172)

7. *BOX 1:* Define the tip-of-the-tongue phenomenon and Brown and McNeill's experiment. What did they conclude from their study? (172)

VERBAL LEARNING

8. Describe the following: (174)

Verbal learning—

Nonsense syllables—

Rote learning—

Ebbinghaus—

Forgetting curve—

9. Define and compare each of the following measures of retention: (175)

Recall—

Recognition—

Relearning—

Savings—

10. *BOX 2:* For the study of "Those Unforgettable High-School Days" identify the test and summarize the results for each of the following: (174)

Free recall—

Picture recognition—

Picture prompting—

11. *BOX 2:* What are the implications of this experiment? What does it indicate about recognition versus recall and the use of visual and verbal coding? (175)

12. Define and distinguish between: (177)

Proactive interference—

Retroactive interference—

13. What are the effects of sleeping during the retention interval? Explain how these results tell us something about interference. (178)

14. Describe the serial position effect. Why does it occur? What does this tell us about interference? (178)

WHY DO WE FORGET?

15. Define retrieval failure. What is meant by *decay* in long-term memory? What does recent research suggest about decay? (178)

16. Describe Tulving's experiment and his conclusions. How can retrieval cues be provided? (179)

17. Define motivated forgetting and repression. What is Holmes' view of repression? (180)

RECONSTRUCTIVE MEMORY

18. How is retrieval reconstructive? Describe the experiment that illustrates reconstructive memory. (180)

MEMORY AND THE BRAIN

19. How did Lashley search for engrams? Did he find any? (181)

20. What is now believed to be the primary physiological mechanism underlying learning? Define consolidation phase. (181)

21. Describe retrograde amnesia as produced by accidents and in the laboratory. How does it illustrate consolidation? (181)

22. *BOX 3:* Describe the effects of puromycin and strychnine on memory consolidation. Why is the application of these findings to human memory still in the future? (183)

DISORDERS OF MEMORY

23. Define, distinguish among, and give the implications of: (182)

Transient global amnesia—

Korsakoff's syndrome—

Case of H. M.—

Case of S.—

IMPROVING MEMORY

24. Define and specify the effects of the following: (186)

Spaced study periods—

Active recitation—

Reviewing—

Giving meaning to material—

25. Define *mnemonic device.* Describe Bower and Clark's experiment and two reasons for the effectiveness of this device. (187)

26. Describe and distinguish the following: (188)

One-is-a-bun system—

Pegword method—

Method of loci—

Keyword method—

27. Summarize the evidence for the method of loci. List three reasons for its success. In general, how does Bower view this method? (188)

PSYCHOLOGICAL ISSUE: *MEMORY AND THE LAW*

28. Summarize the findings from two classroom demonstrations of the reliability of eyewitness testimony. What is imaginative reconstruction? (192)

29. Summarize the results from three studies by Elizabeth Loftus. (193)

30. What is a stacked lineup? What makes them unfair? (194)

Self-Quiz

1. Unless we keep repeating it, something in short-term memory will have disappeared after about:
   a. 1 second.
   b. 20 seconds.
   c. 4 minutes.
   d. 8 minutes. (Study Question 2)

2. Transfer of material to long-term memory depends most upon:
   a. recognition and relearning.
   b. recall and encoding.
   c. rehearsal and encoding.
   d. relearning and recall. (Study Question 3)

3. Which of the following statements is true?
   a. Most of the research on remembering and forgetting has employed psychoanalytic techniques.
   b. The use of nonsense syllables in studies of memory was popularized by Ebbinghaus within the last ten years.
   c. Learning which does not involve meaning is called rote learning.
   d. All of the above are true. (Study Question 8)

4. The measure of retention that shows the greatest retention after a long period of time is:
   a. recall.
   b. recognition.
   c. relearning.
   d. repression. (Study Question 9)

5. You learn a song with a similar tune to one you have learned before. You find that when you try to hum the new song you confuse it with the old one. This is an example of:
   a. proactive interference.
   b. retroactive interference.
   c. hyperactive interference.
   d. radioactive interference. (Study Question 12)

6. If you memorize the list 7, 4, 6, 8, 3, which number is most likely to be forgotten?
   a. 7
   b. 6
   c. 8
   d. 3 (Study Question 14)

7. Memories that are related to emotional conflicts and which might produce severe anxiety cannot be recalled because of:
   a. interference.
   b. long-term decay.
   c. repression.
   d. retrograde amnesia. (Study Question 17)

8. Human memory can be improved by all of the following *except:*
   a. relearning and overlearning.
   b. systematic encoding.
   c. keyword systems.
   d. memory drugs. (Study Question 22)

9. The inability to hold any information in memory storage for more than a few seconds has been called:
   a. retrograde amnesia.
   b. transient global amnesia.
   c. amnesia plus fugue.
   d. apnea. (Study Question 23)

10. Spring ahead; fall back. This saying helps one to remember which way to turn the clock from saving to standard time. This is an example of:
    a. chunking.
    b. a mnemonic device.
    c. eidetic imagery.
    d. consolidation. (Study Question 25)

Answers to Self-Quiz: 1.b 2.c 3.c 4.c 5.a 6.b 7.c 8.d 9.b 10.b

Programmed Review Unit

SHORT-TERM AND LONG-TERM MEMORY

sensory/fraction of a second
meaning
short
chunks
seven

1. Most of the incoming stimulations are held in a stage of ________ storage, which lasts a ________. Information that has some ________ goes on into ________ -term memory. The STM can be increased if you organize input into ________. The STM of a normal person can handle ________ such pieces of information. (168)

12
20
repeating

2. Short-term memory begins fading after ________ seconds, and has disappeared entirely after ________ seconds unless we kept ________ the material to ourselves. (169)

rehearsal
encoding
meaningful

3. The two basic processes by which we get information from short-term memory into long-term memory are (a) ________ (repeating it to yourself or keeping a picture of it in your mind) and (b) ________ it (linking it to concepts and categories you have already learned). Of these two, encoding in a ________ way is the most important. We need to carefully code material in meaningful

categories

clusters or ________, such as vegetables, metals, people, etc., which is easier to remember than nonsensical information. (171)

retrieval
cues

4. One way to improve information ________ is to encode it carefully in the first place. Retrieval is also facilitated by using ________, or reminders, that you can associate with the material to be retrieved. (172)

VERBAL LEARNING

meaning
speaking/writing
recognize

5. Brown and McNeill's (1966) research indicates that our verbal storage system is cross-referenced by both ________ and ________. The meaning-filing system helps us find the right word when ________ or ________, while the sound-filing systems helps us to ________ and understand words. (173)

WHY DO WE FORGET?

rapidly
learning

6. Ebbinghaus's forgetting curve shows that forgetting occurs ________ at first. He also found that the greater the degree of the original ________, the greater the retention. (176)

cues
recognition
relearning
savings
most

7. In recall the individual must reproduce something previously learned with the help of only the barest of ________. Our ________ of people or events tends to be easier than our recall. That is one reason why correctly filling in this programmed review (a check of your recall) makes taking a multiple-choice quiz (a test of recognition) seem easier. In the third measure of retention, namely ________ ability, the difference between the first and second learnings is the ________ in trials or time. This method of retention is ________ able to detect retention over long periods of time. (175)

earlier
later
retroactive
sleeping

8. In proactive interference, material learned ________ interferes with retrieval of something learned ________. When a newly learned information hinders the recall of information that was learned previously, ________ interference has occurred. The effects of retroactive interference can be reduced by ________ between learning and recall. (177)

age
recognition
visual/verbal

9. Free recall of high-school classmates declined steadily with ________, while subjects did much better on picture and name ________ tests; we need to enter our mental filing system with the proper ________ or ________ cues. (175)

rehearse
middle

10. Interference may be explained by the need to ________ material in order to get it in long-term memory. The serial position effect says that you will have the hardest time remembering the ________ part of a list, which may be blocked by both proactive and retroactive interference. (177)

not true
locate
cues
unfinished

11. Recent research indicates that the statement "for every addition of knowledge you forget something you knew before" is ________. Tulving (1974) suggests that much of forgetting is actually a failure to ________ information that is in one's memory; this forgetting results from a lack of the ________ needed to retrieve the information. The Zeigarnik effect says we tend to recall ________ tasks. (179)

12. We can forget information because we ________ to forget it. This is related to Freud's concept of ________, whereby we are unable to retrieve some memories, because they are related to ________ conflicts. Holmes (1974) suggests that forgetting is not caused by repression but rather by emotional interference when the material is learned that keeps us from paying ________ to the material. (180)

[**want**, **repression**, **emotional**, **attention**]

RECONSTRUCTIVE MEMORY

13. Sulin and Dooling (1974) found that people could be influenced by different backgrounds into "recognizing" a sentence they had ________ seen before. (181)

[**never**]

MEMORY AND THE BRAIN

14. You need a period of time, called the ________ phase, for chemical changes to have a permanent effect on the brain. This may explain why people who suffer brain injury or are given ________ experience amnesia for the events just ________ the injury or shock. The drug puromycin ________ the consolidation of memories. On the other hand, the drug ________ improves memory consolidation. At the moment, all of the drugs that affect memory in animals either are ________, addictive, or lead to convulsions. (181)

[**consolidation**, **electroconvulsive shock**, **before**, **blocks**, **strychnine**, **poisonous**]

DISORDERS OF MEMORY

15. In transient global amnesia a person cannot hold on to any information for more than a ________. In Korsakoff's syndrome, which results from excessive intake of ________, the person is ________ unable to place new information in long-term storage. (182)

[**few seconds**, **alcohol**, **permanently**]

16. Luria's famous subject S. remembered every concrete experience, but could not ________ across situations, which prevented him from holding any job that required him to organize, ________, or evaluate. (185)

[**generalize**, **classify**]

IMPROVING MEMORY

17. Good study strategies include ________ study periods, because long study periods make it harder for you to encode the material in a ________ way. One method of rehearsal is active ________, which focuses your ________ on the material at hand; this improves your ability to ________ (not merely recognize) the material when needed. ________ material follows the principle of savings. The most important of all study strategies is giving ________ to the material, which is much more efficient than ________ learning. (186)

[**spacing**, **meaningful**, **recitation/attention**, **recall**, **Reviewing**, **meaning**, **rote**]

18. One illustration of the value of meaningful organization was shown in Bower and Clark's (1969) study in which subjects using the narrative method recalled ________ percent of all the words, while subjects in the control group recalled only ________ percent. The narrative method also adds vivid ________ images to the material to be recalled. Pavio (1971) found that ________ is

[**94**, **14**, **visual**, **recall**]

verbal — best when you use both the visual and ________ coding
processes at the same time, because they bring both brain
hemispheres — ________ into play. (187)

pegs — **19.** Words in a rhyme serve as ________ to which images of the
word to be learned are attached. The method of loci depends on a vivid
locations — image of a set of familiar ________. In one study the method of
loci resulted in better recall (compared to a control group) after one week
92 — (________ percent versus 64 percent) and after five weeks (80
36 — percent versus ________ percent). The key word method can
foreign language — be effectively used to learn a ________; subjects using this
28 — method had 88 percent correct recall versus ________ percent
for subjects who learned by rote. (188)

PSYCHOLOGICAL ISSUE: *MORALITY AND THE LAW*

unreliability — **20.** Illustrating the ________ of eyewitness testimony,
60 — ________ percent of the witnesses, including the professor,
failed to pick the professor's assailant from a set of six photographs;
25 — furthermore, ________ percent of the students identified an
innocent bystander as the assailant. In criminal proceedings, it is often
incorrectly assumed that memory is complete, easily
accessible/accurate — ________, and totally ________. Loftus (1974)
found that subjects who viewed videotapes of cars that "smashed" were
faster — more likely to recall the cars traveling at ________ speeds and
glass — producing broken ________ than students who saw the same
videotape, but were told the cars "contacted" each other. (192)

21. A witness may very easily make a mistaken identification if he or she is
biased — asked to select a suspect from a lineup that is ________ in
particular ways. In another study, even when it was proved that the
single eyewitness had 20/400 vision and was not wearing glasses at the
68 — time, ________ percent of student-jurors voted to convict a
defendant in a murder case. (194)

Self-Quiz

1. The key to getting something from short-term memory into long-term memory is:
a. retrieval.
b. rehearsal.
c. the reticular activating system.
d. recognition.

2. The key to retrieval of information is:
a. a long short-term memory.
b. good organization at the time of registration.
c. sufficient serotonin in the brain.
d. a visual filing system.

3. Which statement is not true of memory?
a. Items are easier to remember if they are meaningful.

b. We have verbal and visual coding abilities.
c. Recall is easier than recognition.
d. Active recitation focuses your attention on the material to be learned.

4. Short-term memory lasts no more than:
a. 20 seconds.
b. 2 minutes.
c. 24 hours.
d. 5 days.

5. The method of measuring retention most effective in detecting long-term retention is:
a. recognition.
b. recall.
c. relearning.
d. hypnosis.

6. Your memory will be improved if you do all but which one of the following?
a. Sleep between learning and recall.
b. Rehearse the information.
c. Study the same amount of time in fewer sessions.
d. Focus attention on the information to be learned.

7. Memory can be impaired as a result of all but which one of the following?
a. Too much memorization.
b. Too much alcohol.
c. An injury to the brain.
d. An electric shock to the brain.

8. Subjects using the narrative method recalled ________________ of the test words, when compared with Bower and Clark's control subjects.
a. half as many
b. the same number
c. twice as many
d. six to seven times as many

9. What percent of the eyewitnesses identified an innocent bystander as the professor's assailant?
a. 0 percent.
b. 2 percent.
c. 10 percent.
d. 25 percent.

10. Which statement is not true of the method of loci?
a. Vivid images of familiar locations are used.
b. One week after using this method people had 28 percent better recall.
c. Five weeks after using this method people had 44 percent better recall.
d. It uses peg words.

Answers: 1.b. 2.b 3.c 4.a 5.c 6.c 7.a 8.d 9.d 10.d

Chapter 7

Language, Thought, and Intelligence

LANGUAGE

1. Contrast learning theorists' view of language with that of the Egyptian king. (197)

2. Summarize Chomsky's position on language development. How does overregularization support Chomsky's contention? (198)

3. *BOX 1:* Specify how baby talk differs from adult speech. Why? What are the reasons adults speak baby talk? (200)

4. Summarize the sequence of language development up to the age of about 9 months. What do Lenneberg's findings reveal? (199)

5. Summarize language development between 9 months and 2 years. Define phoneme and overextension. (199)

6. Summarize language development from age 2 onward. What distinctive characteristic of language emerges? (201)

7. Explain the differences in the style (referential and expressive) and sequence of language development. (201)

8. Describe critical periods in relation to language development. (202)

9. Why don't chimps speak? Describe the accomplishments of Washoe. Why do critics not consider apes to be language users? (202)

10. Describe Terrence's study, his conclusions, and the criticisms of his findings. (203)

CONCEPTS

11. Define: (205)

Concept—

Positive instance—

Negative instance—

Prototypical example—

Carmichael, Hogan, and Walter's study—

12. What are the functions of concepts? What did Rosch find about prototypical objects? What is meant by levels of generality and how do they change with age? (205)

13. How are concepts affected by culture, experience, and needs? Define stereotype. (208)

PROBLEM SOLVING

14. Describe categorization, trial and error, and insight in problem solving. Summarize Köhler's experiments. (208)

15. Define functional fixedness. What evidence shows that scientists can suffer from it? (209)

INTELLIGENCE

16. What is the key feature of most definitions of intelligence? What problem does this raise for intelligence testing? (211)

17. *BOX 3:* Why were intelligence tests greeted with enthusiasm? Why have group intelligence tests been banned in some schools? (212)

18. *BOX 3:* Why are IQ tests thought to be discriminatory? How well do they predict success in school and other areas of life? (212)

19. *BOX 3:* How would McClelland and Cronbach solve the problems of IQ tests? (212)

20. Describe: (211)

Binet and Simon—

Mental age—

Intelligence Quotient—

Adult IQ—

Stanford-Binet test—

21. Describe: (213)

Wechsler—

WAIS—

WISC—

22. Define standardization and normal curve. Summarize the odds of having a given IQ. (214)

23. Summarize the positions of Spearman and Thurstone on intelligence. Describe the compromise position. (215)

24. Describe the information-processing approach to intelligence and the three components noted by Sternberg. (215)

25. Describe Sternberg's experiments and his view of intelligence. (215)

26. Define heritability. How is the heritability of IQ determined by studies of twins? What is the estimate of the heritability of IQ? (216)

27. Describe Skeel's study. What does it demonstrate? (217)

28. Summarize social-class and racial differences in IQ. How have these differences been accounted for? (218)

29. Describe the studies by Scarr and Weinberg and by Jensen. (218)

EXTREMES OF INTELLIGENCE

30. Define mental retardation. Note the varieties of retardation, including Down's syndrome. Describe four classifications of retardation. (219)

31. Define clinical retardation. (219)

32. Define sociocultural retardation. Summarize the attempts to prevent it through early intervention. (219)

33. What is the problem of labeling people retarded? (220)

34. Define mainstreaming and normalization. (220)

35. How is eminence related to intelligence? Describe the method of Terman's study and the results related to the two purposes of the study. (221)

36. What is being done for gifted children today? (221)

PSYCHOLOGICAL ISSUE: *CREATIVITY*

37. How is creativity related to mental problems? Summarize each of the four stages of the creative process. (225)

38. Summarize Amabile's research on creativity. When do external rewards foster creativity? (225)

39. Characterize each of the following kinds of children according to Wallach and Kogan's research: (227)

High creativity, high intelligence—

Low creativity, high intelligence—

High creativity, low intelligence—

Low creativity, low intelligence—

Self-Quiz

1. The idea that humans have an innate capacity to use language is associated with:
a. Noam Chomsky.
b. Sigmund Freud.
c. B. F. Skinner.
d. E. L. Thorndike. (Study Question 2)

2. Which of the following is not true?
a. Infants with two deaf parents babble no differently than infants with normal parents.

b. Most babies babble by 6 months of age.
c. The noise level of the home does not have much effect on infant babbling.
d. Chinese babies babble less but speak sooner than American babies. (Study Question 4)

3. Children whose style of language was largely expressive would be most likely to say which of the following?
a. "Pretty."
b. "Mommy."
c. "Give."
d. "I." (Study Question 7)

4. Carmichael, Hogan, and Walter's study demonstrated:
a. a homonymic response.
b. semantic generalization.
c. the effect of language on perception.
d. the effect of learning on language. (Study Question 11)

5. Köhler put a basket out of reach of some apes, but with one way to get to the basket. The apes seemed to solve the problem suddenly, and they used that solution every time from then on. This was a demonstration of:
a. inductive reasoning.
b. deductive reasoning.
c. insight.
d. trial and error. (Study Question 14)

6. If a 7-year-old child has a mental age of eight years, what is her IQ?
a. 87.
b. 97.
c. 114.
d. 120. (Study Question 20)

7. Spearman's *g* factor refers to:
a. the separate abilities that make up intelligence.
b. intelligence being a single entity.
c. a test taker's generalization ability.
d. the general extraneous factors, other than ability, that affect performance on an IQ test. (Study Question 23)

8. Skeels's study of orphans rated as retarded and placed in a ward with older retardates demonstrates:
a. the strong influence of heredity on intelligence.
b. that a warm and stimulating environment can dramatically increase one's IQ.
c. the debilitating effect of being with retardates in early life.
d. a stimulating and loving environment can only temporarily increase one's IQ. (Study Question 27)

9. Terman's study of gifted children noted that, compared to a control group, his subjects were in general:
a. healthier, better adjusted, and superior in moral attitude.

b. weaker, more introverted, and superior in moral attitude.
c. weaker, unhealthy, and inferior in moral attitude.
d. higher in incidence of death, alcoholism, and illness. (Study Question 35)

10. Children who are most distressed over making a mistake in the classroom tend to fall into which category?
a. High creativity, high intelligence.
b. Low creativity, high intelligence.
c. High creativity, low intelligence.
d. Low creativity, low intelligence. (Study Question 39)

Answers to Self-Quiz: 1.a 2.d 3.c 4.c 5.c 6.c 7.b 8.b 9.a 10.b

Programmed Review Unit

thinking
language

1. The mental manipulation of ideas— ________ — is inseparable from the set of symbols we use for communicating ideas— ________. (196)

LANGUAGE

operant
content
innate
imitation
overregularize

2. Learning theorists believe language is learned behavior that is developed through use of ________ conditioning. However, there is little evidence that the ________ of infants' babblings is strongly affected by direct reinforcement. Chomsky (1969) argues that people's capacity for language is ________. Evidence for Chomsky's contention that language is not just a matter of ________ and reinforcement is revealed in children's tendency to ________ rules of language: e.g., "I *maked* my bed." (198)

6
12
18/24
4½

3. Children in most any culture begin to babble at about age ________ months, say their first word at about ________ months, and begin to combine words when they are ________ to ________ months old. By the age of ________ the average child has learned the basic grammar of adult speech. (199)

higher

4. Babies prefer sounds in ________ pitch ranges, which not only helps them learn to talk, but expresses affection in ways normal speech cannot. (200)

phonemes
names
2
five

5. At around 9 months the infant's babbling narrows. She or he begins to distinguish the recognizable sound units of a language, which are called ________. The baby's first words are typically ________; such words are often overextended to many objects. At about age ________ children form their first two-word sentences. Expanding to age 6, children learn an average of ________ new words a day. (199)

referential

6. Some children are primarily ________, using words to label

expressive
mother's

objects while others are primarily ________________, using words to express desires; these preferences may reflect their ________________ verbal style. (202)

2/14

7. Lenneberg (1967) suggests that the critical period for language development goes from ages ________ to ________. (202)

sentences/create
imitation
nonhumans

8. Washoe the chimp produced sequences of signs that resembled ________________, and seemed to ________________ expressions. On the other hand Terrence (1979) believed that Nim's language could be accounted for in terms of prompting and ________________ of his trainers. At present there is no clear consensus that ________________ can or cannot learn language. (202)

CONCEPTS

grouping
common
examples
positive/negative

9. A concept is a mental ________________ of a set of objects or events on the basis of important ________________ features. Most concepts are learned from ________________ of those concepts. Concepts can be either ________________ or ________________. (205)

label or category

10. The Carmichael, Hogan, and Walter (1932) study shows that the ________________ we give to an object influences the way we see and remember the object. (206)

Prototypical

11. ________________ examples contain especially typical characteristics of an object. (205)

appropriately
generality
older

12. Concepts help us only if they ________________ organize our experience. We also categorize objects at different levels of ________________, as instances of either more inclusive, broader categories or narrower, more specific categories. Brown (1958) notes that children learn more specific levels of generality as they get ________________. (207)

culturally
objectively
groups
stereotypes

13. Because classifications are socially and ________________ determined, there is no ________________ correct way to classify most of the objects in our experience. Concepts about whole ________________ of people—which are often inappropriate to any particular person—are called ________________. (207)

PROBLEM SOLVING

categorize

14. Deciding how to ________________ a problem is often the first step towards its solution, as illustrated by deciding whether a problem is one of addition or multiplication. (208)

trial/error
simple/Insight
functional fixedness
old
habitual or ingrained
flexible

15. The process of ________________ and ________________ involves trying each of many solutions one by one and is useful in solving ________________ problems. ________________ into one problem often leads to solutions for similar problems. On the other hand, we demonstrate the difficulty of ________________ when we try solutions that worked for ________________ problems instead of discovering more appropriate solutions. Rigidity in thinking may result from using ________________ ways of thinking or behaving. Instead, we need to be ________________ in our approach to solving problems. (209)

INTELLIGENCE

capacity **use** **words/numbers** **grades**	**16.** Intelligence is the ________ to acquire and ________ knowledge. IQs are based on people's performance on measures of their skill, that particularly involve the ability to manipulate ________ and ________. Whereas IQ scores are related to school ________, there is a raging controversy about their relevance to people's capacity to acquire and apply knowledge in other areas of life. (210)
adults **112**	**17.** The MA/CA formula is not used for ________. An 8-year-old with a mental age of 9 would have an IQ of ________ (9/8 × 100). (211)
validity/predict **school** **learning**	**18.** Some parts of the United States have banned standardized group intelligence tests from schools because of doubts about their ________. IQ tests are still used to ________ success in ________. Some psychologists believe that IQ tests are useful in diagnosing ________ problems. (212)
verbal **similarities/memory** **performance** **individually**	**19.** The Stanford-Binet test relied heavily on ________ skills, while the Wechsler intelligence scales differentiate between verbal tests (such as word ________, vocabulary, and ________ span) and ________ tests (such as picture completion, picture arrangement, and object assembly. Both the Wechsler and Stanford-Binet tests are administered ________. (213)
representative **bell**	**20.** The standardization of intelligence tests consists of administering it to large, ________ samples of people. The resulting distribution of their scores usually forms a normal ________ -shaped curve. (213)
1 **3** **80**	**21.** Approximately ________ percent of Terman and Merrill's 1960 sample had IQs of 140 and above, while ________ percent had IQs of 69 and below. About ________ percent of all people will fall between 80 and 119. (214)
general **independent**	**22.** Intelligence seems to include a ________ ability that underlies scores on a wide variety of subtests. There also seem to be clusters of intellectual abilities that are ________ from one another. (215)
processes **encode** **infer** **apply** **more**	**23.** More recently, some researchers have shifted their attention to the step-by-step ________ people use in assessing information. Sternberg (1979) notes that the first step, or component, is to ________ the information of, for example, an analogy problem. Then the person must ________ the relationship between the first two terms of the analogy, and finally ________ the relationship to the second half of the analogy. Sternberg noted that people with high IQs take ________ time to perform the first step, encoding. (215)
heredity **environment** **similarities** **kinship** **40 to 60** **identical**	**24.** Intelligence seems to be a product of both ________ and ________. Heritability is calculated on the basis of the ________ between the traits of individuals who stand in different degrees of ________ to one another. It is generally estimated that heredity accounts for about ________ percent of the variation in people's IQ scores, which is supported by evidence that the IQs of ________ twins are more similar than any other pairs of siblings. (216)

retarded
happiness
28
loss
more

25. The fact that the environment influences intelligence is shown by the Skeels (1966) study in which orphans rated as retardates were lodged with ________________ adults who provided love, attention, and stimulation. The children improved in health and ________________, and showed an average IQ increase of ________________ points, while retarded children in a control group (living in the orphanage) showed an IQ ________________ of from 8 to 45 points. Thirty years later the two groups were ________________ different than before. (217)

15
earlier
affluent/higher
educationally
decline

26. There is evidence that, on the average, the IQ of blacks is about ________________ points lower than that of whites. Scarr and Weinberg (1976) found that the ________________ in life black children moved from impoverished environments to the homes of ________________ white families the ________________ their IQs tended to be. Jensen (1977) found that if black children remained in economically and ________________ disadvantaged environments their IQs tended to ________________. (218)

EXTREMES OF INTELLIGENCE

70
135

27. People with IQs lower than ________________ are often regarded as mentally retarded, and those with IQs above ________________ are regarded as intellectually gifted. (218)

55
physical/cannot
25
sociocultural
educationally/malnutrition
stimulation/encouragement

28. Clinical retardation (IQ of less than ________________) usually has a ________________ cause, and ________________ be treated effectively. Down's syndrome accounts for ________________ percent of these cases. Unlike clinical retardation, cases of ________________ retardation tend to be from families that are economically, socially, and ________________ disadvantaged. Disease, ________________, environmental hazards such as lead-paint poisoning, and lack of intellectual ________________ at home or ________________ to succeed in school are factors that contribute to sociocultural retardation. (219)

26
normal
mothers

29. Five years of efforts to stimulate the language learning, problem solving, and motivation to learn and achieve in children of retarded women showed these children had an average IQ of ________________ points higher than children of mothers with ________________ IQs who had not received such help. Sometimes, though, the ________________ lost interest in the program. (220)

mainstreaming
normalization

30. The current trend of ________________ allows retarded students to attend regular classes; this contributes to the ________________ of the lives of retarded individuals. (220)

135
adjusted
school

31. Terman studied 1528 children with IQs of ________________ or higher, and found that they were healthier, better ________________, and more advanced in mastery of ________________ subjects than children in the control group. (221)

PSYCHOLOGICAL ISSUE: *CREATIVITY*

disturbed
preparation

32. Few truly creative people are seriously ________________. The four stages in the creative process are (in order) (a) ________________, (b)

incubation/illumination
verification
insight
least

rewards/grades

intrinsically

______________, (c) ______________, and (d) ______________. The periods of incubation and illumination are identical to the process of ______________ in normal problem solving. Amabile (1979) believes we are ______________ likely to be creative when we expect our work to be evaluated, and when we are working to gain financial ______________, high ______________, or the approval of others. Instead, we are most likely to be creative when we are ______________ motivated. (225)

low
high

33. Wallach and Kogan (1967) found that the children least likely to engage in disruptive classroom activities were the ______________ creativity-______________ intelligence children. (227)

Self-Quiz

1. Which one of the following characteristics of creativity is/are similar to the process of insight in normal problem solving?
a. Preparation and verification.
b. Incubation and illumination.
c. Originality.
d. Productivity.

2. Which statement is not true?
a. Stereotypes are concepts about whole groups of people.
b. Most concepts are learned from examples.
c. We can objectively classify most objects in our experience.
d. Concepts are mental groups of sets of objects or events that have important common features.

3. If a 5-year-old has the mental age of a 7-year-old, she would have an IQ of:
a. 100.
b. 120.
c. 140.
d. 170.

4. When we try to fit new problems into improper, formerly used categories, we are demonstrating:
a. insight.
b. stereotyping.
c. functional fixedness.
d. trial and error.

5. Which one of the following statements is not true of linguistic development?
a. Skinner believes that language is learned through classical conditioning.
b. Children say their first word at about one year of age.
c. Chomsky believes that our capacity for language is innate.
d. Chomsky believes we learn linguistic rules.

6. Which one of the following statements is not true of linguistic development?
   a. Children begin to babble at about 4 months of age.
   b. Children begin to combine words between 18 and 24 months of age.
   c. Children learn basic adult grammar by 4½ years of age.
   d. The child's first word is usually a name.

7. Which one of the following does not characterize the Wechsler intelligence scales?
   a. There are eleven subtests.
   b. They rely heavily on verbal skills.
   c. Word similarity and vocabulary tests are included.
   d. Object assembly and picture completion are included.

8. Children who remained in the orphanage in the Skeels study:
   a. remained at the same retarded IQ level.
   b. showed a loss of nearly 8 to 45 IQ points.
   c. showed slight IQ changes that were nonconsistent.
   d. showed an average increase of 28 IQ points.

9. A person is more likely to be creative if he or she is all but which one of the following?
   a. Energetic.
   b. Productive.
   c. Original.
   d. Mentally disturbed.

10. In previous research the average IQ of blacks has been:
    a. the same as that of whites.
    b. about 5 points above that of whites.
    c. about 5 points below that of whites.
    d. about 15 points below that of whites.

Answers: 1.b 2.c 3.c 4.c 5.a 6.a 7.b 8.b 9.d 10.d

Chapter 8

Motivation

1. Define motive. Distinguish among survival, competence, and social motives. (231)

THE SURVIVAL MOTIVES

2. List the four most important survival motives. What do they have in common? (232)

3. Define the following: (232)

   Need—

   Drive—

   Goal—

   Drive reduction theory—

4. Describe Cannon's theory of hunger and the two problems with it. (232)

5. Describe two functions of the hypothalamus in regulating eating. What happens when the hypothalamus is destroyed? (232)

6. Define hyperphagic. What role does taste play in hyperphagic animals? How is this related to obesity in humans? (233)

7. *BOX 1:* List two explanations for obesity. Describe the Stunkard and Koch experiment. What does it illustrate? (236)

8. *BOX 1:* Summarize Schachter's evidence concerning taste, visibility, and time in overeating. What general conclusions can be drawn? (236)

9. How does the strength of the thirst drive compare to the strength of the hunger drive? (234)

10. Describe the evidence that dryness of the throat is not the only factor in thirst. How else is thirst controlled physiologically? (235)

11. What are the effects of sexual abstinence? Describe the strength of the sex drive, how it is controlled in lower animals, and how it differs for humans. (235)

THE COMPETENCE MOTIVES

12. Define master reinforcer and competence motives. List two reasons why the authors feel that these motives are not drives. (238)

13. Summarize the evidence for curiosity and exploration motives. Describe Berlyne's theory. (239)

14. Define sensation-seeking motive and Zuckerman's theory about it. (240)

15. Define the concepts of cognitive consistency and cognitive dissonance. How can cognitive dissonance be reduced? (241)

16. How is cognitive dissonance related to other motives? Describe Mansson's experiment. (242)

17. *BOX 3:* What are cognitive motives? What is the strongest form of such cognitive motivation? (243)

18. Define the need for control. What does Brehm mean by psychological reactance, and how is this concept illustrated by Worchel and Arnold's study? (243)

19. Define learned helplessness and give the evidence that supports the concept. How is it related to reactance? (244)

20. Why is the need for control important for older people? Describe Langer and Rodin's study. How can feeling helpless make one feel better? (245)

UNCONSCIOUS MOTIVES

21. Define: (246)

Repressed motives—

Incest taboo—

Freudian slips—

22. *BOX 4:* List (from the bottom up) the categories of needs in Maslow's hierarchy. How do people go about satisfying these needs? Define self-actualization. (247)

MOTIVES IN CONFLICT

23. Use the terms goal and motive to define each of the following: (248)

Approach-approach conflict—

Approach-avoidance conflict—

Avoidance-avoidance conflict—

PSYCHOLOGICAL ISSUE: *WORK AND ACHIEVEMENT*

24. Define intrinsic and extrinsic motivation. Describe Deci's experiment and his conclusions. (254)

25. How does McClelland measure achievement motivation? Summarize the findings on achievement motivation. (255)

26. What are the effects of achievement-motivation training? What are Spence and Helmreich's conclusions about competitiveness? (256)

27. Describe Horner's concept of the motive to avoid success. How have the findings of studies of this motive changed recently? (257)

Self-Quiz

1. Drive reduction theory suggests that motives start as:
a. psychological needs.
b. psychological drives.
c. physiological needs.
d. hyperphagic drives. (Study Question 3)

2. The regulatory mechanism for hunger resides in the:
a. bloodstream.
b. cerebral cortex.
c. gonads.
d. hypothalamus. (Study Question 5)

3. In the Schacter, Goldman, and Gordon taste-test experiment, which of the following was not found?
a. Normal-weight subjects ate fewer crackers when their stomachs were full.
b. Normal-weight subjects ate more crackers when their stomachs were full.
c. Overweight subjects ate just as much or slightly more when their stomachs were full.
d. Eating behavior of overweight subjects has little to do with the condition of their stomachs. (Study Question 8)

4. The experience of thirst is related to the:
a. level of salt in the bloodstream.
b. level of sugar in the bloodstream.
c. water level in the stomach.
d. volume of blood circulating through the body. (Study Question 10)

5. The drive reduction theory can not explain:
a. hunger motive.
b. thirst motive.
c. sex motive.
d. competence motives. (Study Question 12)

6. The need for cognitive consistency (consonance) is not associated with which of the following statements?
   a. It may have strong inhibitory influence over the physiological need to drink water.
   b. It represents a desire to minimize inconsistencies between our attitudes and our behavior.
   c. It can be exemplified by a heavy smoker thinking of a dozen people who smoked heavily and lived long lives.
   d. It is a healthy defense mechanism which makes for effective interaction with the environment just as other competence motives do. (Study Questions 15 and 16)

7. The theory that explains the effectiveness of "reverse psychology" is the theory of:
   a. cognitive dissonance.
   b. learned helplessness.
   c. psychological reactance.
   d. drive reduction. (Study Question 18)

8. After basic survival and security needs are met, Maslow suggests that we are motivated by the need for:
   a. love and belonging.
   b. self-esteem.
   c. self-actualization.
   d. exploration. (Study Question 22)

9. You didn't want to study last night but you didn't want to flunk today's quiz either. This was what kind of conflict?
   a. Approach-approach.
   b. Approach-avoidance.
   c. Avoidance-avoidance.
   d. Escape-approach. (Study Question 23)

10. Research on the achievement motive has shown that:
   a. the strength of the achievement motive seems to be equally strong in all cultures.
   b. a high need for achievement in adulthood is correlated with independence training in childhood.
   c. there is little relationship between childhood experiences and later need for achievement.
   d. a high need for achievement and dependency in childhood are positively correlated. (Study Question 25)

Answers to Self-Quiz: 1.c 2.d 3.b 4.a 5.d 6.d 7.c 8.a 9.c 10.b

Programmed Review Unit

causes
move
survival
competence

1. The ________________ for a person's behavior are called motives, which come from the Latin word for "________________." The two types discussed in this chapter are ________________ motives and ________________ motives. (230)

THE SURVIVAL MOTIVES

reduction **need** **drive/sugar** **hypothalamus** **fat** **cognitive**	**2.** In drive ________________ theory, motivation begins with a physiological ________________, which is experienced as a psychological ________________. When blood ________________ is low, the ________________ causes one to feel hungry and eat more; this organ tries to inhibit us from eating when the ________________ content of the body goes above a certain point. Among humans, ________________ factors—thoughts, attitudes, and values—have a great deal to do with eating behavior. (232)
Thirst **salt** **hypothalamus**	**3.** ________________ seems to be an even stronger motive than hunger and is linked to the level of ________________ in the bloodstream, which in turn sends messages to the ________________ to activate the thirst drive. (234)
10 to 25 **internal** **taste** **visibility** **normal** **unrelated** **over** **cause or cure** **external**	**4.** Dieticians estimate that from ________________ percent of the U.S. population is overweight. Normal-weight people seem to regulate the amount they eat through ________________ cues, such as how hungry they feel. Overweight people seem to respond more to external cues, such as the ________________ of food, its availability, and its ________________. Stomach contractions and reports of hunger closely coincided for ________________ -weight people only. The eating behavior of overweight people was ________________ to the condition of their stomachs. A phony lapse of time stimulated eating more among the ________________ -weight people. Rodin (1979) emphasizes that obesity has no single ________________, but the Schachter studies suggest that if you are overweight you should avoid ________________ food cues. (236)
no good **testosterone/estrogen** **no clear** **Psychological** **social**	**5.** There is ________________ evidence that abstinence from sexual activity is detrimental to a person's health. Among lower mammals, such as rats, sexual behavior is strongly controlled by the sex hormones ________________ in the male and ________________ in the female. In humans, there is ________________ evidence for a relation between hormone level and sexual desire. ________________ and ________________ motives play a large role in regulating sexual behavior. (235)

THE COMPETENCE MOTIVES

competence **curiosity or exploration** **consistency/control** **drive**	**6.** White (1959) defines ________________ as a person's capacity to interact effectively with the environment. Competence motives include the ________________ motive, the need for cognitive ________________, and the need for ________________ over the environment. The notion of ________________ doesn't seem to be the most useful way of viewing competence motives. (238)
exploring **unfamiliar** **sensation** **hereditary**	**7.** Much of what we call "play" in children is a way of ________________ the environment. Berlyne (1967) believes that exploring the ________________ tends to increase our degree of arousal, which we don't want to be too great or too little. Zuckerman (1980) believes that the level of a person's ________________ -seeking motive may be determined in part by biological factors. A recent study of twins suggests that sensation seeking may have a large ________________ component. (240)
attitudes **actions**	**8.** The phrase cognitive dissonance refers to our discomfort when we perceive inconsistencies between our ________________, or between these and our ________________. We are motivated to

change ________ one or the other. Dissonance reduction
does not ________ make for effective interaction with the environment. (240)

threatened 9. The motive to restore or reassert a ________ freedom is called
reactance psychological ________. (243)

cognitive 10. Competence motives may also be characterized as ________ motives, as exemplified by ideologies. (243)

helplessness 11. Seligman (1975) suggests that learned ________ may be the result of experiences in which we repeatedly find ourselves unable to
control ________ the outcome. People, who because of past experience, don't expect to control their outcomes are
less ________ likely to experience reactance and will give up more quickly. Langer and Rodin (1976, 1977) found that when old people were encouraged to take control over their environment, they had increase in
morale/activity ________, ________ level, and
lifespan ________. (244)

UNCONSCIOUS MOTIVES

12. Freud believed certain of our emotions are repressed, or banished from
consciousness/anxiety ________ because they are too ________ -arousing for us to deal with. (246)

13. Maslow's pyramid of human needs includes (from the most primary going up):
physiological (a) the basic ________ needs of food, water, and sex;
safety (b) the need for ________ and security; (c)
love/esteem ________ and belonging needs; (d) self- ________
actualization needs; and (e) self- ________ needs, which is the need to
capacities or talents realize one's ________. (247)

MOTIVES IN CONFLICT

14. If two of your favorite TV programs are on at the same time, you are
approach-approach probably experiencing an ________ - ________ conflict. And if you have to choose between two unattractive candidates in an election you are experiencing an
avoidance/avoidance ________-________ conflict. In an
goal approach-avoidance conflict there is one ________ but two
motives ________. As you get closer to the goal, the
avoidance ________ tendency gains in strength. (248)

PSYCHOLOGICAL ISSUE: *WORK AND ACHIEVEMENT*

three 15. Most adult Americans spend at least one of every ________ waking hours working. The many motives for working include the
ideas opportunity to learn or use new ________ and the opportunity
socialize to ________. Of the people who were asked what they would do if they inherited enough money to let them stop working, about
80 ________ percent said they would continue working anyway. One-third of the respondents said that joblessness would make them feel
lost ________. (252)

16. When you do an activity for the pleasure of it, you are
intrinsically ________ motivated, because the activity is its own
reward ________. If you are working for money or good grades or
punishment/extrinsically avoidance of ________, you are ________ motivated. Subjects who were paid spent significantly

less	________ time than subjects who worked the same puzzles for
decreased	free: intrinsic motivation ________ when subjects were given
reward	an external ________. (254)
achievement	**17.** People's ________ motivation has been measured by the
Thematic Apperception	stories they produce about a series of pictures called the ________ Test. McClelland (1953) believes that people's
fantasies	________ provide a less direct, but more useful measure than answers to a questionnaire. McClelland also found that the amount of
children's	achievement imagery in ________ textbooks in the 1920s was related to the economic development in various countries
20	________ years later. (255)
	18. Spence and Helmreich believe achievement motives include: (a) work
hard	orientation—the desire to work ________ and do a
good	________ job; (b) mastery—a preference for
difficult or challenging	________ tasks; and (c) ________, which is
competitiveness	particularly *low* in the ________ achievers. (256)
highest	
decreased	**19.** In the past decade fear of success has ________ in women. (257)

Self-Quiz

1. Which one of the following statements is false?
- **a.** Women have become more fearful of success in the last decade.
- **b.** Men have become more fearful of success in the last decade.
- **c.** Horner suggests that women may see success as unfeminine.
- **d.** Mothers of achievement-oriented boys expected them to do things for themselves at an early age.

2. Which one of the following statements is false?
- **a.** Eighty percent of workers said they would continue to work even if they didn't need to.
- **b.** The highest achievers are high in competitiveness.
- **c.** The amount of achievement imagery in children's textbooks is related to a country's economic development 20 years later.
- **d.** One of the motives for working is the opportunity to learn new ideas.

3. Dieticians estimate that at least ________ of the American public is overweight.
- **a.** 3 percent
- **b.** 5 percent
- **c.** 10 percent
- **d.** 25 percent

4. Which one of the following is the next-to-highest need in Maslow's pyramid?
- **a.** Physiological needs.
- **b.** Self-actualization needs.
- **c.** Self-esteem needs.
- **d.** Love and belonging needs.

5. Which one of the following statements is not true of learned helplessness?
   a. It may be the result of experiences in which we have too much control.
   b. People who can't control the outcome may experience reactance.
   c. When old people were given a plant that they took care of, they had a higher activity level.
   d. When old people were given a plant that they took care of, they lived longer.

6. Which statement is not true?
   a. Abstinence from sexual activity is detrimental to a person's health.
   b. As you get closer to the goal, the avoidance tendency gains strength.
   c. There is no clear relation between hormone level and sexual desire in humans.
   d. The strongest survival motive is thirst.

7. Which one of the following statements is not true of eating behavior?
   a. Overweight people regulate eating through internal cues such as how hungry they feel.
   b. Overweight people respond more to taste and visibility of food.
   c. A phony lapse of time affected overweight people more than normal-weight people.
   d. Stomach contractions coincided with reports of hunger more often in normal-weight people.

8. Competence motives include all but which one of the following?
   a. Curiosity.
   b. Need for cognitive consistency.
   c. Need to reduce physiological drives.
   d. Need for control over the environment.

9. Which one of the following statements is not true of motivation?
   a. When you do an activity for the pleasure of it, you are intrinsically motivated.
   b. When you are working for money or good grades, you are extrinsically motivated.
   c. Intrinsic motivation increases when people are given extrinsic motivation.
   d. McClelland believes that people's fantasies reveal their achievement motivation.

10. Which one of the following statements is not true?
   a. Freud believed some emotions are repressed because they are too anxiety arousing.
   b. Much of play is a way of exploring our environment.
   c. Old people had higher morale if they had more control over their environment.
   d. Dissonance reduction is an effective way of dealing with the environment.

Answers: 1.a 2.b 3.c 4.c 5.a 6.a 7.a 8.c 9.c 10.d

Chapter 9

Emotion and Stress

1. List the components that must be considered in defining emotion. (259)

THE PHYSIOLOGY OF EMOTION

2. List the similarities in the physiological responses associated with fear and anger. (260)

3. List the physiological differences between fear and anger that were found by Ax. What is the function of these bodily reactions? (262)

4. *BOX 1:* Define GSR and PSE. List four problems in lie detection. How accurate is the polygraph? (261)

THEORIES OF EMOTION

5. List the three factors involved in emotions. According to the James-Lange theory, how are they related to each other? (262)

6. Describe the primary weakness of the James-Lange theory. How does this lead to the Cannon-Bard theory? Describe the Cannon-Bard theory. (263)

7. Describe the cognitive labeling theory of emotion. Note how it is related to earlier theories. (264)

8. Describe the method, predictions, results, and conclusions of the Schachter and Singer study. (264)

9. *BOX 2:* Describe the role of labeling in the experience in love. How does Schachter's theory account for the results of the Dutton and Aron study? (268)

10. What is facial feedback theory? How was it anticipated by James? What are the implications for controlling feelings? (267)

11. Describe the Lanzetta et al. and the Tourangeau and Ellsworth experiments and the implications of each for facial feedback theory. (268)

EVOLUTION AND EMOTIONAL EXPRESSION

12. Describe Darwin's view of emotional expression. What kind of recent evidence supports this view? (269)

13. Describe the studies of Ekman. What conclusion does Ekman draw from these data? (270)

THE DEVELOPMENT OF EMOTION

14. Compare the old view of emotional development (exemplified by Bridges) with the view of Izard. (272)

15. Describe Saarni's study and the conclusions from it. (273)

16. What are the roles of learning and biological predispositions in the development of fear. Describe the conditioning of Little Albert. What does it show? (273)

17. Distinguish between fear and phobia. How are childhood fears related to socioeconomic background. How does culture influence fear? (274)

18. *BOX 3:* What three things have led scientists to suspect that hormonal changes cannot explain the emotional and physical responses to menstruation? (276)

19. *BOX 3:* List the ways in which cultural beliefs and negative expectations may contribute to negative menstrual experiences. (274)

WHEN EMOTIONS DESTROY: THE CASE OF STRESS

20. List the three stages of response to stress according to Selye. (276)

21. What is the relationship between emotional stress and various diseases? Define psychosomatic disease. (277)

22. What is the incidence of ulcers in air traffic controllers? What two factors produce stress in controllers? How does this stress produce ulcers? (278)

23. How does social support reduce stress? How is the endocrine system involved? (279)

24. Describe the method and results of Brady's executive monkey study. (279)

25. Describe the method and results of a similar study by Weiss. Why were the results different from Brady's? (280)

26. Describe the evidence that shows how control and prediction reduce stress. When does control fail to reduce stress? (281)

27. Define life crisis. Give some examples of both positive and negative events. (282)

28. What is the evidence for the relation between life-change experiences and illness? How might stress cause illness or death even when an individual appears to be coping with it? (283)

29. How is stress related to psychological functioning and socioeconomic status? (283)

PSYCHOLOGICAL ISSUE: *VIOLENCE*

30. Summarize Lorenz's argument on aggression and list three objections to it. (286)

31. Summarize the frustration-aggression hypothesis and the qualifications of it that must be made. (287)

32. Define catharsis. Discuss the evidence with respect to catharsis. (288)

33. What were the results of the Bobo doll experiment? In what two ways does observing violence produce violence? Do these effects occur outside the laboratory? (288)

34. Summarize the Drabman and Thomas study. What does it illustrate? (289)

35. Define institutional violence. Summarize Zimbardo's prison study. (290)

Self-Quiz

1. Which of the following is not considered a major component of the definition of emotion?
a. Physiological changes.
b. Perceptual reorganization.
c. Expressive behavior.
d. Subjective feelings. (Study Question 1)

2. Which of the following physiological changes typify anger to a greater degree than fear?
a. Greater increases in blood pressure.
b. Greater increases in heart rate.
c. Greater increases in muscle tension.
d. Greater increases in sweat gland activity. (Study Question 3)

3. The theory of emotion which suggests that we feel sorry because we cry and angry because we strike out is the:
a. Cannon-Bard theory.
b. Selye theory.
c. James-Lange theory.
d. cognitive labeling theory. (Study Question 5)

4. In Schachter and Singer's study, the subjects who attributed their arousal to an emotion relevant to the social situation in which they found themselves were the:
a. epinephrine informed group.
b. epinephrine uninformed group.
c. epinephrine group.
d. placebo group. (Study Question 8)

5. In the Dutton and Aron (1975) study, a greater sexual response was elicited by an attractive female experimenter when she confronted males who were:
a. crossing a fear-arousing bridge.
b. crossing a solid bridge.
c. passing through a dark subway.
d. passing through a lighted subway. (Study Question 9)

6. When Ekman showed pictures of American facial expressions to a New Guinea tribe, the Fore, he found that:
a. they had considerable difficulty in matching expressions with emotions.
b. they were generally quite accurate in matching pictures with emotions.

c. they confused fearful expressions with angry expressions.
d. they confused angry expressions with surprise expressions. (Study Question 13)

7. According to Selye, the three stages in the stress reaction are:
a. alarm reaction, exhaustion, resistance.
b. alarm reaction, resistance, exhaustion.
c. resistance, exhaustion, alarm reaction.
d. resistance, alarm reaction, exhaustion. (Study Question 20)

8. The executive monkeys studied by Brady and the executive rats studied by Weiss:
a. both showed more effects of stress than their control partners.
b. showed very different reactions.
c. both showed fewer effects of stress than their control partners.
d. had to work extremely hard in order to attain their executive positions. (Study Question 25)

9. Lorenz's argument that aggression is natural has been criticized because:
a. some human cultures have been found with very little violence.
b. there are large individual differences in aggressiveness.
c. chimpanzees and many other species of animals are naturally quite peaceful.
d. all of the above. (Study Question 30)

10. The statement that violence breeds violence is best supported by:
a. the frustration-aggression hypothesis.
b. catharsis theory.
c. the concept of aggressive modeling.
d. the theory of displacement. (Study Question 33)

Answers to Self-Quiz: 1.b 2.a 3.c 4.b 5.a 6.b 7.b 8.b 9.d 10.c

Programmed Review Unit

physiological/subjective
expressive

1. Some psychologists characterize emotion as the reflection of ________ changes in our bodies, as the ________ feelings we experience, or as the ________ behavior that we exhibit. (259)

THE PHYSIOLOGY OF EMOTION

180
rapid/blood pressure
anger
sympathetic
stop
up/sugar
fats

2. When you are emotionally aroused, your heart may accelerate to as much as ________ beats per minute, your breathing may become ________ and uneven, and your ________ may rise. Both fear and ________ are controlled by the ________ branch of the autonomic nervous system, which will cause the movements of your stomach and intestines to ________, your body's metabolism rate to go ________, and the ________ in your bloodstream and the ________ in your tissues to be burned off at a faster

salivary
sweat
pupils
anger

rate. Your ________________ glands will stop working, while the opposite will be true of your ________________ glands, and your ________________ may enlarge. Both fear and anger raise blood pressure, with increases greatest during ________________. (260)

THEORIES OF EMOTION

are not
bodily
can
behavior

3. Both the James-Lange theory and the Cannon-Bard theory of emotion ________________ accepted today. The James-Lange theory states that the experience of emotion results from the perception of one's ________________ changes. There is evidence that we ________________ gain control over our emotions by altering our ________________. (263)

dry
sweat
is not
voluntary

4. Emotional tension may produce a ________________ mouth. The galvanic skin response is a measure of ________________, which is produced in greater quantities by people in highly emotional states. The evidence to date suggests that the Psychological Stress Evaluator ________________ reliable as a lie detector. Lie detection is based on physiological reponses that are, to some extent, under ________________ control. (261)

cognitive labeling
precede
similar/situation
decides
context

5. The theory of emotion now being debated by psychologists is Schachter's ________________ theory, which, like the James-Lange theory, says that bodily changes ________________ the experience of emotion. The person looks at the patterns of physiological arousal which are quite ________________, and depending on the ________________ in which the arousal occurs, he or she ________________ which particular emotion he or she is feeling. In the Schachter and Singer (1962) study, subjects tended to attribute their arousal to an emotion that was appropriate to the social ________________ they were in. (264)

fear
Schachter's

6. In the Capilano Canyon study, subjects apparently relabeled their inner stirrings of ________________, at least in part, as sexual arousal and romantic attraction, which supports ________________ theory. (266)

facial
less
fewer
did not

7. Izard (1977) believes that our awareness of our own ________________ expressions is a primary ingredient in our experience of emotion. Researchers found that subjects who suppressed their fear and pain reported that they felt ________________ upset, and they showed ________________ physiological signs of arousal than did the subjects who expressed their feelings. The evidence found by Tourangeau and Ellsworth (1979) ________________ support the facial feedback theory of emotion. (268)

EVOLUTION AND EMOTIONAL EXPRESSION

inborn

8. Recent evidence supports Darwin's contention that particular emotional expressions are ________________ and universal across cultures. (269)

THE DEVELOPMENT OF EMOTION

excitement
smiling/distress
experience

9. Bridges (1932) thought that at birth the only apparent emotion is one of unfocused ________________. In contrast, Izard (1978) believes that newborns have distinctive emotional expressions: startle, ________________, disgust, ________________, and interest. It remains debatable whether infants actually ________________ a wide range of emotions. (272)

learn
experience
conditioned

10. In general, we ________ to be fearful as a result of both cultural teachings and our own ________. Watson and Rayner (1920) ________ Albert to be afraid of furry things. (273)

WHEN EMOTIONS DESTROY: THE CASE OF STRESS

environment
emotional
alarm
resistance/exhaustion

11. Stress is pressure from our ________ that makes physical and ________ demands on us. According to Selye (1956), the three stages of stress are (a) the ________ reaction, (b) the stage of ________, and (c) the stage of ________. (275)

cultural
hormone
more

12. The recent evidence suggests that women attribute many discomforts to their menstrual cycle as a result of ________ beliefs rather than fluctuating ________ levels. When women in one study were told the research concerned menstruation, they reported ________ cyclical symptoms than women who were not told the purpose of the study. (276)

physical
third/air traffic
uncertainty
social support

13. Numerous ________ problems are caused at least in part by stress. At least one-________ of the ________ controllers in the United States suffer from ulcers, which seems to come from constant vigilance and ________. House and Wells (1978) found that the effects of stress can be reduced through adequate ________. (279)

executive
control group
less
successful/relax

14. In the four pairs of monkeys, the ________ monkeys developed severe ulcers and died, while the ________ monkeys survived. In the experiment in which the executive rat could control its environment sufficiently to prevent shocks being given to it and its control-group rat, the average executive rat had much ________ ulceration than its helpless partners. Weiss (1972) believes that the difference between the findings of the monkey and rat studies can be explained by how certain the animal is that its efforts will be ________; the executive rat could ________ until after the next beep. (279)

control
predictable

15. Glass and Singer (1973) found that merely knowing that one could ________ a noise seems to make it less bothersome. Even when we cannot control them, unpleasant events also seem less stressful if they are ________. (281)

spouse
jail
injury/illness
reconciliation
90
illnesses

16. The top ten life crises, according to Holmes, are: (1) death of ________, (2) divorce, (3) marital separation, (4) ________ term, (5) death of close family member, (6) personal ________ or ________, (7) marriage, (8) fired from job, (9) marital ________, and (10) retirement. In the first month of a Navy cruise, the men who had been exposed to severe life changes before embarking had nearly ________ percent more ________ than the low-risk group. (282)

depression
aggression
poor

17. Stressful life events produced feelings of ________, paranoia, ________, anxiety, distress, and tension. Stress may account for the higher incidence of depression among the ________. (283)

PSYCHOLOGICAL ISSUE: *VIOLENCE*

doubled
tripled
highest

18. Between 1960 and 1978, the murder rate in the United States almost ________ and the overall violent crime rate ________; the homicide rate in the United States is one of the ________ in the world. (286)

ethologist
survival
cultures

19. Konrad Lorenz, an ________ (student of animal behavior) believes that humans are violent because violence was useful for ________. But this explanation does not account for the fact that there are some ________ in which there is very little violence. (286)

goal/Aggression
displaced
for
submission/avoidance

20. Frustration is caused by the blocking of efforts to attain some desired ________. ________ may be directed toward the person who caused the frustration, or it may be ________ toward an innocent bystander. There is a great deal of evidence ________ the frustration-aggression hypothesis, but it does not seem to be universal. Among the Kwoma of New Guinea, frustration may lead to aggression, or it may lead to dependence, ________, and ________. (287)

observe
no
most

21. Berkowitz (1973) found that the more we ________ violence, the more likely we are to behave aggressively in the future. There is ________ evidence that aggressing has a cathartic effect. Those cultures with the most aggressive games and sports tend to be the ones that are ________ involved in aggression. (288)

aggression
acceptable
new
less
more
roles
brutal
sadistic

22. Children's nonimitative ________ suggests that observing violence can have far-reaching effects. The aggressive model seems to make a wide range of aggressive behaviors more ________ to children. Observing violence also teaches children ________ ways to be violent. As juveniles and adults, the more we see or read about violence, the ________ it seems to bother us. The third- and fourth-graders who watched a violent movie took ________ time to call for help in breaking up a fight than did children who hadn't seen the movie. Violence may be encouraged by people's ________ in certain large organizations or social institutions. In Zimbardo's (1974) experiment, well-adjusted college students randomly assigned to be prison guards exhibited ________ and ________ behavior. (289)

Self-Quiz

1. At least ________ of the air traffic controllers in the United States suffer from ulcers.
   a. one-tenth
   b. one-fourth
   c. one-third
   d. one-half

2. The average executive rat had ________ ulceration when compared to the average yoked rat.
   a. less
   b. slightly more
   c. an equal amount of
   d. three times as much

3. Which of the following can be used to reduce stress?
   a. Control the event.

b. Know that you could control the event, but not attempt to change it.
c. Predict the event.
d. All of the above.

4. Which one of the following is not in the top ten life crises?
a. Marriage.
b. Visit by in-law.
c. Retirement.
d. Marital reconciliation.

5. Both fear and anger are controlled by the ________________ nervous system.
a. somatic
b. central
c. sympathetic
d. spinal

6. Which one of the following statements is not true of fear and anger?
a. Blood pressure is raised.
b. Heart rate increases more during anger.
c. Sweat production increases more during fear.
d. Muscle tension increases more during fear.

7. Which one of the following statements is not true?
a. We can gain control over our emotions by altering our behavior.
b. There is evidence that each emotion has its own unique pattern of bodily changes.
c. The James-Lange theory states that our experience of emotion results from perceiving bodily changes.
d. Evidence does not support the facial feedback theory of emotion.

8. Which one of the following statements is not true of stress?
a. The executive monkeys suffered more than the helpless monkeys.
b. The executive rats suffered less than the helpless rats.
c. Animals suffered less if they could relax.
d. Unpleasant events are more stressful if we can predict them.

9. Which statement is not true?
a. In 1977 there were over a million violent crimes in the United States.
b. Violence is universal across cultures.
c. Depression may be the result of stress.
d. Depression is more common in poor people.

10. Which statement is not true?
a. Aggressing will not have a cathartic effect.
b. Cultures with aggressive sports have the most wars.
c. Well-adjusted college students assigned to be prison guards remained fair and nonaggressive.
d. The polygraph demonstrated 92 percent accuracy in locating the guilty person.

Answers: 1.c 2.a 3.d 4.b 5.c 6.b 7.b 8.d 9.b 10.c

Chapter 10

Personality

1. Define personality. What are the two goals of the study of personality? (292)

2. Define and distinguish: (293)

   Idiographic approach—

   Nomothetic approach—

FREUD'S PSYCHOANALYTIC THEORY

3. Summarize the general biological-motivational and developmental focuses of Freud's theory. (294)

4. *BOX 1:* Describe the events that led Freud from the practice of neurology to psychiatry. How did his practice lead to his theory of repression? (294)

5. *BOX 1:* List two of Freud's early publications. How were they received? How did he rise to prominence? (294)

6. Define and distinguish among the following terms: (296)

Id—

Ego—

Superego—

Erogenous zone—

Psychosexual stages—

Fixation—

7. Describe the oral and anal stages. What results from successful or unsuccessful passage through these stages? (297)

8. Describe: (298)

Phallic stage—

Oedipus complex—

Castration anxiety—

Electra complex—

Penis envy—

9. Define latency period and genital stage. (300)

10. Define and show the relationship between: (300)

Anxiety—

Defense mechanism—

11. Define, distinguish, and give examples of: (301)

Repression—

Projection—

Reaction formation—

Displacement—

Rationalization—

Intellectualization—

12. Summarize the difficulties in evaluating Freud's theory scientifically. (302)

13. Summarize the authors' evaluation of Freud's theory. (303)

THE PSYCHOANALYTIC DISSENTERS

14. Define: (303)

Jung—

Personal unconscious—

Collective unconscious—

15. Outline Adler's theoretical position. (304)

16. Define neo-Freudians. List four of them and their major ideas. (304)

TYPE THEORIES

17. Define type theory. List four basic types described by Hippocrates. What notion of his persists? (305)

18. Summarize Sheldon's type theory. List and describe the three somatotypes and their associated personality types. (305)

19. Summarize Jung's type theory. How does it differ from other type theories? (306)

20. Describe two major criticisms of type theories. (306)

TRAIT THEORIES

21. What is the goal of trait theories? What three measurement techniques do they typically employ? (307)

22. Describe Allport's trait theory. Distinguish common and individual traits. (307)

23. Summarize the studies of the development of traits. (307)

24. *BOX 2:* Describe: (308)

Personality inventories—

MMPI—

Projective tests—

TAT—

Rorschach—

THE ISSUE OF CROSS-SITUATIONAL CONSISTENCY

25. What is the issue of cross-situational consistency? What kinds of theories hold this assumption? (309)

26. Describe the Hartshorne and May study. What conclusion can be drawn from it? What is Mischel's conclusion? (310)

27. Describe the study of Bem and Allen. On the basis of all the evidence, what can be concluded about cross-situational consistency? (311)

SOCIAL LEARNING THEORY

28. Describe social learning theory. How is it influenced by Skinner? (312)

29. Describe the role of generalization and discrimination in explaining cross-situational consistency and inconsistency according to social learning theory. (313)

30. How does social learning theory go beyond Skinner's formulation? What is the major criticism of social learning theory and Mischel's answer to it? (313)

31. *BOX 3:* Distinguish between internal and external control. Summarize two studies that reveal differences between internals and externals. (315)

32. Describe the development of locus of control and the advantage of internality. (315)

HUMANISTIC THEORIES

33. Define humanistic theories. Describe Rogers' theory with regard to self-concept, unconditional positive regard, and incongruence. (316)

34. *BOX 4:* Define self-esteem. Summarize the difference between high and low self-esteem boys and the differences between their parents. What did Coopersmith conclude? (317)

35. Summarize Maslow's theory of personality and define the concepts of self-actualization and peak experiences. (318)

PSYCHOLOGICAL ISSUE: *MORALITY*

36. Describe and distinguish between: (321)

Moral realism—

Moral independence—

37. Summarize Kohlberg's extension of Piaget's analysis of moral reasoning. (322)

38. Describe Candee's study of the Watergate figures. (325)

Self-Quiz

1. A research strategy that aims at understanding the uniqueness of an individual is called the:
a. nomothetic approach.
b. personality testing approach.
c. experimental approach.
d. idiographic approach. (Study Question 2)

2. According to Freud, the moral part of the personality is the:
a. ego.
b. superego.
c. id.
d. Oedipus. (Study Question 6)

3. Freud's anal stage is essential to the development of:
a. trust.
b. pity.
c. love.
d. flexibility and generosity. (Study Question 7)

4. Freud thought most adult personality problems:
a. stem from unrealistic expectations for one's self.

b. stem from general feelings of inferiority.
c. stem from fixations and other problems that occur in early childhood.
d. stem from complexes and fixations that occur mostly in the late teens and early adulthood. (Study Questions 3 and 9)

5. A sexually frustrated male sees the secretaries in his office as forever making passes at him. He is most likely using which defense mechanism?
a. Displacement.
b. Reaction formation.
c. Projection.
d. Rationalization. (Study Question 11)

6. Jung's concept that part of the human psyche is filled with primordial images or archetypes is called the:
a. unconscious function.
b. psychic unconscious.
c. subconscious.
d. collective unconscious. (Study Question 14)

7. According to Sheldon, an extremely thin person would be expected to have a personality that is:
a. ectomorphic.
b. mesomorphic.
c. endomorphic.
d. pseudomorphic. (Study Question 18)

8. Personality tests which assess personality do not include:
a. MMPI.
b. TAT.
c. PKU.
d. Rorschach. (Study Question 24)

9. Hartshorne and May provided children with opportunities for different types of immoral acts (lying, stealing, and cheating) in many different settings. They found that:
a. children who were immoral in one setting were the ones most likely to be immoral in all other settings.
b. a child who stole at home was no more likely to do other types of acts than any other child, but would be more likely to steal in other settings.
c. a child who stole at home was no more likely to steal in other settings than any other child, but would be more likely to do other types of immoral acts in the home setting.
d. there was very little consistency in children's immoral behavior either between types of immoral behavior or between settings. (Study Question 26)

10. The theorist who is responsible for the notion that humans pass through a hierarchy of needs to self-actualization is:
a. Carl Rogers.
b. Abraham Maslow.

c. Erich Fromm.
d. Carl Jung. (Study Question 35)

Answers to Self-Quiz: 1.d 2.b 3.d 4.c 5.c 6.d 7.a 8.c 9.d 10.b

Programmed Review Unit

behavior
emotions
adaptation
idiographic
patterns

1. Personality refers to the distinctive patterns of ________, thoughts, and ________ that characterize the individual's ________ to the situations of his or her life. The focus on the detailed study of individuals is called the ________ approach to personality, while attempts to discover general ________ of personality reflect a nomothetic approach to personality. (292)

FREUD'S PSYCHOANALYTIC THEORY

instinctual
sexual
unconscious
subdue
emotional
death
fully formed

2. Freud believed that a person's behavior is motivated by ________ biological urges, which are primarily ________ and aggressive. Even though these impulses are repressed and become ________, they continue to dominate our personality. The need to ________ these impulses inevitably leads to ________ conflicts. In Freud's later work, the ________ instincts (including aggression) held a place in prominence equal to that of sex. Freud believed that the personality is almost ________ by the time a child enters school. (294)

biological
ego
socially
conscious
executive
destructive
values
parents
ideal/ought to be
id

3. The id, according to Freud, is the reservoir of basic ________ urges. Its insistent demands are moderated by the ________. The ego controls the id by requiring it to seek gratification within ________ acceptable bounds, and unlike the id, most of the ego's actions are ________. The ego acts like an ________ who sees to it that the gratification of impulses will not be painful, dangerous, or ________ to the organism. The superego is the force within the self that acquires the ________ and ideals of ________ and society. The superego looks to the ________ rather than the real, to what ________ rather than what is, and limits the impulses of the ________. (296)

Hysteria
temporarily
catharsis
free association

4. ________ is an emotional disorder in which people suffer physical symptoms without any discernible physical basis; hypnosis helped ________. The expression of bottled up emotions is called ________. Saying whatever comes to mind is called ________. (294)

gratification
fixated
oral
dependence/trust

5. If a person gets either too much or too little ________ of his or her sexual impulses in a particular psychosexual stage, he or she may become ________ at that stage. In the first stage, the child's erogenous zone is his or her ________ area. Psychologically, at this time the child is dealing with oral gratification, personal ________, and ________ in others. In the second stage, the __________ stage, the major psychological issues involve giving and __________, cleanliness and __________, and dominance and __________. The __________ complex occurs, according to Freud, during the __________ stage. At this stage, boys develop a __________ anxiety. Freud hardly thought about the psychological development of __________ until after he worked out the Oedipus cycle. Sexual urges are __________, Freud believed, from the end of the phallic stage until __________, at which time the __________ stage began. Freud's analysis of adult problems almost invariably presumed __________ at the earlier stages. (297)

anal
holding back
messiness/subservience
Oedipal
phallic
castration
females
latent
puberty
genital
fixations

6. Freud believed that anxiety stemmed from our unconscious fear that our __________ will cause us to do something that we will be __________ for. Defense mechanisms first __________, falsify, or distort reality, and second, operate __________. The most basic and most common defense mechanism is __________, which is the exclusion of unacceptable unconscious impulses from __________. The unconscious attribution of one's own thoughts and feelings to others constitutes the defense mechanism of __________. Reaction formation is the development of behavior patterns that are __________ of those that might create anxiety. When the object that will gratify an instinctual urge is inaccessible, __________ may occur. Another common defense mechanism is __________, which occurs when we attempt to substitute "good" reasons for our __________ reasons. Through intellectualization, anxiety is dismissed by analyzing __________ issues intellectually and converting them to theory rather than __________. The use of defense mechanisms to deal with anxiety and conflict may be __________. (301)

instincts
punished/deny
unconsciously
repression
consciousness
projection
opposite
displacement
rationalization
real
emotional
action
costly

7. It is not easy to evaluate Freud's psychoanalytic theory __________; his theory does not __________ events ahead of time. (302)

scientifically/predict

THE PSYCHOANALYTIC DISSENTERS

8. Unlike Freud, __________ distinguished two levels of the unconscious: (1) the __________ unconscious, which encompasses repressed or forgotten material; and (2) the __________ unconscious, a universal part of the human psyche that is filled with primordial images, or __________. Jung believed that these unconscious forces, if properly used, are a central part of the __________ personality. (303)

Jung
personal
collective
archetypes
healthy

9. Adler focused on the effects of feeling __________. (304)

inferior

10. Erich Fromm, Karen Horney, and Erik Erikson, as examples of __________-Freudians, gave less emphasis to __________ drives and __________ stages of development, and more emphasis to the influence of __________. (304)

neo
instinctual/fixed
society or culture

TYPE THEORIES

type **irritable/depressed** **optimistic/listless**	**11.** Hippocrates proposed an early and primitive ________ theory of personality, which was that there were four basic temperaments: choleric (________), melancholic (________), sanguine (________), and phlegmatic (________). (305)
sensitive **mesomorphs** **endomorphs** **skeptical**	**12.** According to Sheldon, ectomorphs are ________, solitary, and cerebral; ________ are assertive, incautious, and independent; and ________ are relaxed, self-indulgent, and approval-seeking. Many psychologists are quite ________ of Sheldon's conclusions. (305)
innate **introversion/extraversion** **dominance**	**13.** Jung believed that every individual possesses ________ mechanisms for both ________ and ________, and that a person becomes a type only if one of the mechanisms wins ________. (306)
little	**14.** Type theories have been of ________ use in the study of personality. (306)

TRAIT THEORIES

trait **common/individual** **combination**	**15.** In contrast to type theories, in which people are assigned to one category or another, ________ theories of personality view people on many dimensions simultaneously. Allport distinguished between what he called ________ and ________ traits, as well as unique ________ of traits for each person. (307)
origins **temperamental** **biological or hereditary** **dependency**	**16.** While concentrating on description and measurement, trait theorists have paid relatively little attention to the ________ of a person's traits. Thomas, Chess, and Birch (1970) believe that there is some degree of consistency between babies' ________ styles ("easy," "slow to warm up," and "difficult") and their styles in childhood and adolescence. These researchers believe that the difference in the babies' dispositions are ________. Dwarkin et al. (1976) believe that anxiety and ________ have at least some genetic basis. (307)

THE ISSUE OF CROSS-SITUATIONAL CONSISTENCY

the same **challenged** **situation**	**17.** Psychoanalytic, type, and trait theories of personality all assume that people have ________ personalities in different times and situations. This assumption of cross-situational consistency has been ________ by a number of studies, which support the possibility that our behavior is often determined by the particular ________. (309)
inventories **emotional/projective** **TAT**	**18.** Techniques for measuring personality traits include personality ________ that attempt to measure interests, ________ styles, and values; and ________ tests on which the person "projects" his or her interpretations of various materials. Projective tests, exemplified by the Rorschach and the ________, sometimes are not reliable. (309)

friendliness
believed
correct
over
small

19. Bem and Allen (1975) found only a small degree of consistency in a person's ________ and conscientiousness across situations. However, people were more consistent if they ________ they were; the students' self-assessments were gradually ________. One reason for our tendency to ________ -estimate the degree of other people's consistency is that we usually see other people in a ________ range of situations. (311)

SOCIAL LEARNING THEORY

behavior
motives
reinforced
generalize
discriminate
positive
modeling
expectations
person

20. Social learning theory focuses directly on people's ________, and is not concerned with underlying ________ or traits. According to this approach, people are most likely to behave in ways that have been ________ in the past; situations, from which we ________ to similar situations. We also learn to ________ between situations in which a particular behavior is likely to be rewarded and situations in which it is not. These two processes suggest that people will only behave consistently across situations to the extent to which similar behavior is expected to have ________ consequences. This theory also extends Skinner's formulation by emphasizing the influence of ________ and how much our behavior is shaped by people's ________ of reward or punishment. Some critics contend that social learning theorists have ignored the ________. (313)

believe or expect
control
information
internal
external
money
internal
illness

21. Rotter (1966) states that people who ________ that they can ________ what happens to them are more likely to do so. People with an internal locus of control are more likely to gather ________ through asking questions. Students who had an ________ locus of control were more likely to be social activists. An ________ locus of control is more likely to develop in people who have little ________, power, or influence. Kobasa (1979) found that executives who had an ________ locus of control were less likely to suffer from stress-related ________. (315)

HUMANISTIC THEORIES

rational
subjective
concept
actualization

22. Humanistic theories of personality see people as ________, and emphasize people's uniqueness and their ________ experience. Carl Rogers emphasizes the importance of self-________ in determining behavior, while Abraham Maslow focuses on self-________. (316)

unconditional
real/ideal

23. Rogers stresses the value of ________ positive regard, and hopes that individuals can overcome incongruence between ________ self and ________ self. (316)

esteem
relationships/conforming
high

24. A positive self-evaluation—or self-________—has been linked to being open to ________, being less ________, and setting ________ goals for oneself. Coopersmith (1968) found

academically/socially
disagreement
criticism
depressed
interest/high
consistent
rewards
time
permissive
feedback
did not
can

that boys with high self-esteem were active, expressive individuals who tended to do well both ________ and ________. They were eager to express opinions, did not avoid ________, and were not overly sensitive to ________. Boys with low self-esteem were often discouraged, ________, and anxious. Boys high in self-esteem had parents who showed much ________ in them, set ________ standards for their sons' behavior, and were ________ in enforcing the rules. These parents also relied on ________ rather than physical punishment as a means of discipline. Parents of low self-esteem boys spent less ________ and attention on their sons, tended to be ________, and yet used harsh punishment; the low self-esteem boys did not get daily ________. Positive self-esteem ________ seem to be related to physical attractiveness, height, social class, and outstanding ability. New learning experiences ________ raise or lower self-esteem. (317)

healthy
accepting
spontaneous
beauty
opinions
guilt
peak

25. Maslow found that psychologically ________ or self-actualizing people were ________ of themselves and others, deeply committed to their work, ________ in the expression of their emotions and appreciation of ________, and relatively unconcerned about the ________ of others. These people also had a noticeable lack of ________, shame, or anxiety. Moments of self-actualization are called ________ experiences. (318)

PSYCHOLOGICAL ISSUE: *MORALITY*

realism
rules
unchangeable/independence
situations
intention
concrete
formal
six
implications
interpersonal
invarying
highest
1
2
punishment
3

26. Piaget proposed the existence of two stages of moral development. In the stage of moral ________, the child accepts ________ given from authority, and believes that the rules are ________. Later, in the stage of moral ________, the child can modify rules to fit particular ________. During the first stage the amount of damage counts more than the child's ________, which is a complex concept that the child understands only as she or he enters the stages of ________ and then ________ operational thought. The first two of the ________ stages of moral reasoning proposed by Kohlberg (1969) are similar to Piaget's. Initially, individuals are oriented to the personal ________ of their behavior and later they become oriented to the ________ implications, as well. Kohlberg believes that these stages form an ________ sequence, but that not all people reach the ________ stages. Some of the men involved in the Watergate affair may have rationalized their participation in terms typical of Stages ________ and ________: they may have burglarized for the sake of money and lied in order to avoid ________. Committing perjury because of group pressure demonstrates Stage ________, while committing crimes to protect "national security" and social order

4	is typical of Stage ________________ moral behavior. Emphasis on constitutional rights and responsibilities is typical of Stage
5	________________ behavior. Student subjects at Stages 3 and 4 were
approve	more likely to ________________ of the acts of the Watergate participants than were subjects at Stage 5. Kohlberg's first stage of
obedience	moral development is orientation to ________________ and
punishment	________________; Stage 2 is shown by an orientation to instrumental
hedonism	________________; Stage 3 people are oriented to interpersonal
concordance	________________; Stage 4 people are interested in the established
social	________________ order; Stage 5 people are oriented toward a social
contract	________________; and the highest stage is an orientation to ethical
principles/authority	________________ which transcend ________________ or
law	________________. (322)

Self-Quiz

1. If you convince yourself you love your father when you really hate him, you are showing the defense mechanism of:
a. projection.
b. reaction formation.
c. displacement.
d. rationalization.

2. The Oedipus complex, according to Freud, occurs in the ________________ stage.
a. oral
b. anal
c. phallic
d. latency

3. Probably the most widely used defense mechanism is:
a. projection.
b. repression.
c. fixation.
d. reaction formation.

4. If, as a psychotherapist, you have sex with a client and convince yourself that it was part of the client's therapy, you are engaging in:
a. repression.
b. reaction formation.
c. rationalization.
d. fixation.

5. Which one of the following is not true of the ego?
a. It makes sure impulses are gratified within socially acceptable bounds.
b. Its actions are usually in our awareness.
c. It operates according to the pleasure principle.
d. It is the executive part of personality.

6. Which one of the following is not true of the superego?
   a. It acquires the values of parents and society.
   b. It is the moral part of self.
   c. It controls the ego.
   d. It looks at what is ideal.

7. Which one of the following is not true of the id?
   a. It is the reservoir of our biological urges.
   b. It is controlled by the superego.
   c. Its actions are usually in our awareness.
   d. It is interrelated with the ego and the superego.

8. Which one of the following is not true of Freud's theories?
   a. Freud's theories have generally not been proven.
   b. The subduing of biological urges cleanses people of emotional conflicts.
   c. The latency period is longer than the first three periods combined.
   d. Freud believed that human behavior was dominated by instinctual urges.

9. Which one of the following is not true of defense mechanisms?
   a. They deny reality.
   b. They attempt to relieve anxiety.
   c. They operate unconsciously.
   d. They are the best ways to deal with reality.

10. Which statement is not true?
   a. Adler focused on man's feeling of inferiority.
   b. Jung stresses the need for balance of conscious and unconscious forces.
   c. Rogers believes we need to achieve congruence of real and ideal self.
   d. Kohlberg believes that the highest stage of ethical development is an orientation toward law and order.

Answers: 1.b 2.c 3.b 4.c 5.c 6.c 7.c 8.b 9.d 10.d

Chapter 11

Beginnings of Life

EVOLUTION

1. How is *Homo sapiens* related to modern apes? What is known from fossil evidence about our ancestors? (328)

2. Explain Darwin's principle of natural selection. (329)

GENETICS

3. Define each of the following terms, specifying the role in heredity: (331)

Gene—

DNA—

Genotype—

Dominant gene—

Recessive gene—

4. Define behavior genetics. Summarize the Stone and the Scarr and Weinberg studies. What is meant by saying that the genetic influence on psychological characteristics is indirect? (333)

5. Describe in detail: (336)

PKU—

Tay-Sachs disease—

Sickle-cell anemia—

Cystic fibrosis—

Down's syndrome—

6. *BOX 1:* Describe the two developments that have made the advance detection of birth defects possible. (334)

7. *BOX 1:* Who are genetic counselors? What is their role and what ethical questions affect their work? (334)

8. Why do genetic defects continue to exist despite natural selection? (336)

CONCEPTION

9. Trace the course of development from conception through the first few days. (337)

10. Distinguish between fraternal and identical twins. What are the odds of a single instance of intercourse leading to conception and pregnancy? List three reasons for infertility. (338)

11. *BOX 2:* Describe: (338)

External fertilization—

Biological engineering—

AID—

Surrogate motherhood—

LIFE BEFORE BIRTH

12. Describe the following, distinguishing them from each other: (340)

Zygote—

Embryo—

Fetus—

Placenta—

Amniotic sac—

13. Describe and distinguish between development in the second and third trimesters. (343)

14. *BOX 3:* Describe three methods of sex selection. What questions have been raised about these techniques? (344)

15. Why might a woman miss her period? Summarize the physical symptoms of pregnancy. (343)

16. Summarize the psychological changes that accompany pregnancy and the contribution of cultural attitudes. (343)

17. How is life satisfaction related to reactions to pregnancy? Summarize what is known about the transmission of emotions to the fetus. (345)

18. Describe sympathetic pregnancy. Summarize the role of the expectant father. (346)

BIRTH

19. Describe labor pains. What is the typical length of labor? Describe childbirth among the Cuna and Siriono Indians. What do the differences indicate? (348)

20. Identify: (349)

Natural childbirth—

Childbirth Without Fear—

Lamaze method—

21. How effective is natural childbirth? What are the effects of medication during delivery? Identify two recent trends in childbirth. (349)

22. Identify *Birth Without Violence* and describe the Leboyer method. (350)

THE NEWBORN CHILD

23. Describe newborns' reflexes, senses, and preferences. (352)

24. When do infants acquire the ability to learn? Describe two experiments by Lipsitt. (352)

25. List the ways in which newborns differ from one another. (353)

26. Describe the newborns' sensitivity to human contact. Summarize the importance of early contact with the mother and father. Why is it controversial? (354)

27. *BOX 4:* What determines whether a premature baby will survive? What modern techniques increase survival rates? How does the development of premature infants compare to full-term infants? (356)

28. *BOX 4:* How does parental interaction with premature infants influence development? Summarize Goldberg's study. (356)

29. Summarize parents' reactions to newborns. (355)

PSYCHOLOGICAL ISSUE: *BIRTH ORDER*

30. What evidence shows differences between first-born and later-born individuals? List the areas in which first-borns or later-borns excel. (360)

31. How are birth order and family size related to intelligence? Describe Zajonc's model and its implications. (362)

32. How is birth order related to affiliation? What is the speculative explanation for this? (362)

33. How does sibling interaction explain older children's sense of competence and younger children's slight advantage in social skills? Summarize research on only children. (363)

34. What do the authors conclude about the inconsistency of results of birth-order studies? (365)

Self-Quiz

1. According to Darwin's principle of natural selection:
a. the diversity of organisms retards evolution.
b. organisms are selected randomly to survive and reproduce.
c. variations are produced directly by the process of natural selection.
d. none of the above. (Study Question 2)

2. The genotype is a person's ________________, while the phenotype is the ________________.
a. genetic make-up; outward expression of the genetic make-up.
b. outward expression of the genetic make-up; genetic make-up.
c. dominant traits; recessive traits.
d. recessive traits; dominant traits. (Study Question 3)

3. Down's syndrome is the result of:
a. both parents having Down's syndrome.

b. poor nutrition during pregnancy.
c. an accidental incorrect distribution of genetic material.
d. oxygen being cut off during labor. (Study Question 5)

4. Twins developing from one zygote are commonly called:
a. fraternal.
b. identical.
c. clones.
d. fetal. (Study Question 10)

5. A fertilized egg is called a:
a. fetus.
b. zygote.
c. placenta.
d. gene. (Study Question 12)

6. Which of the following is not a physical symptom of pregnancy?
a. Drowsiness.
b. Nausea.
c. Vomiting and aversion to food.
d. Loss of body water. (Study Question 15)

7. Siriono Indian girls for whom birth is an open, public event have labor that is:
a. extremely short by Western standards.
b. longer, but less painful than in Western cultures.
c. extremely long and difficult by Western standards.
d. not significantly different than labor in Western cultures. (Study Question 19)

8. The ability to learn:
a. is present from birth on.
b. begins when the baby is about 2 weeks to 1 month old.
c. begins around 4 months of age.
d. begins around 9 months of age. (Study Question 24)

9. First-borns are overrepresented among:
a. astronauts.
b. female strippers.
c. eminent scientists.
d. all of the above. (Study Question 30)

10. Zajonc's theory of birth-order effects predicts that:
a. quintuplets should be more disadvantaged intellectually than triplets.
b. a second child should be more disadvantaged than a child with several older siblings.
c. children of one-parent families ought to be more intellectually advantaged than those of two-parent families.
d. none of the above. (Study Question 31)

Answers to Self-Quiz: 1.d 2.a 3.c 4.b 5.b 6.d 7.a 8.a 9.d 10.a

Programmed Review Unit

EVOLUTION

Answers	
	1. The basis of Darwin's account of the variation between and within species
selection	is the principle of natural ________. (329)

GENETICS

Answers	
	2. The carrier of genetic information is a chemical called
DNA	________. The gene for brown eyes is said to be
dominant/recessive	________, while the gene for blue eyes is ________.
randomly	Which gene is included in the sex cell is ________ determined.
	Human traits that are controlled by a single gene pair include
blood/color	________ type, ability to see ________, and hair
curliness/color/ Most	________ and ________. ________
	human traits involve many gene pairs. The genes of two parents can
infinite	arrange themselves in an almost ________ number of
	ways. (331)
less	**3.** Gray rats are ________ easily tamed than white rats because
no	of genetic differences. There is ________ evidence that a
	particular emotional trait can be inherited, but the general tendency to
occupational	be emotional may be inherited. Grotevant et al. (1977) suggest that
people	shared genes may account for similarities of ________
	interest. But genes don't produce behavior—________
	do. (333)
40	**4.** Genetic disorders may account for about ________ percent of
80	infant deaths and ________ percent of all cases of retardation.
	Most genetically caused disorders, such as phenylketonuria, are
recessive	________ genetic traits. Children born with PKU lack an
	enzyme needed to break down an amino acid found in
protein	high-________ foods such as milk; without this enzyme the
builds up	amino acid ________ in the body and eventually destroys cells
brain/retardation	in the ________, producing mental ________,
skin	hyperactivity, ________ disorders and discoloration, and
controlled	epileptic-like seizures. This disease can be ________ with early
blood	discovery through a sample of the ________ from the
Jews	newborns. Tay-Sachs disease only affects ________ from
8/10	Eastern Europe. About ________ to ________
	percent of American blacks are carriers for the defective
sickle-cell	________ gene; and about ________ percent have
	two defective genes and therefore suffer from this painful blood disease,
fatal	which is ultimately ________. Cystic fibrosis affects Northern
whites	European ________. (335)
not	**5.** Down's syndrome is ________ inherited, and occurs at the
conception	time of ________; the probability of having a child with this
mother/older	problem increases as the ________ gets
	________. (336)

amniocentesis

6. The presence of possible genetic diseases in a fetus can be detected through ________. (334)

CONCEPTION

two/five
two
ninety
identical/six

7. Sperm live from ________ to ________ days, while the egg lives no longer than ________ days. Twins occur in about one out of ________ births. One-third of all twins are ________. About one in ________ couples have difficulty in conceiving. (337)

LIFE BEFORE BIRTH

10,000
20,000

8. Every year in the United States some ________ to ________ children are born as a result of artificial insemination. (338)

temperature
shocks/six

9. In the first month after conception, the new organism increases to nearly 10,000 times its initial size. The embryo floats in the amniotic sac, which maintains an even ________ and protects against ________. A baby delivered at ________ months might survive. (340)

rubella
tobacco/alcohol

10. Some maternal infections, such as ________, may be transmitted across the placental barrier, within the first three months of pregnancy. Poor nutrition, certain medications, and even common drugs such as ________ and ________ can harm the unborn child. (342)

faster
boy/female
before

11. Male-producing sperm move ________ than female-producing sperm; having intercourse at the time of ovulation favors the conception of a ________. Because ________ -producing sperm live longer, having intercourse two or three days ________ ovulation favors the conception of a girl. (344)

illnesses
emotional
20/40
six
eight
emotions
avoid

12. A woman may miss her period because of various ________ and ________ upsets, as well as for no apparent reason when she is under ________ or over ________. Morning sickness may occur during the first ________ to ________ weeks of pregnancy. The entire course of pregnancy is likely to be characterized by strong ________. Taylor and Langer (1977) believe that people ________ a pregnant woman, partly because she is a novel sight. (343)

nervous
depressed/does
rest
diet
epinephrine
heartbeat

13. Women who want the pregnancy, have a good marital relationship, and are satisfied with their work are less likely to be ________ and ________ during pregnancy. Evidence ________ support the idea that the woman's moods affect the unborn child's; this may result from the anxious woman getting less ________, or being careless about her ________. When the animal mothers are stressed, increased ________ goes into the bloodstream of the fetus. The infant may also hear the speed of the mother's ________. The infant may match its own activity to the

sleep	mother's ________ and activity cycle both before and after birth. (345)

BIRTH

15 8 expected 1/3 fear relaxation classical actively complications	**14.** The period of labor averages about ________ hours in a woman's first pregnancy, and about ________ hours in later ones. In contrast to the Cuna Indians, among the Siriono Indians of Bolivia, labor and pain is ________ to be minimal—and labor averages ________ to ________ hours. Dick-Read states that labor pains are the result of muscular tensions brought about by ________ in the expectant mother. The Lamaze method teaches the woman to associate ________ of abdominal muscles with uterine contractions through the use of ________ conditioning principles. There is evidence that if a woman has a positive attitude toward pregnancy and participates ________ in delivery, she will have fewer ________. (348)
behavior	**15.** Brackbill (1978) found that 1-year-olds whose mothers had received medication during labor performed less well on standard tests of ________. (349)
dimly silent breathing	**16.** Leboyer advocates delivering babies in ________ lit, ________ rooms, and not cutting the umbilical cord until the baby is ________. (350)

THE NEWBORN CHILD

vision high/moving sweet learning activity	**17.** With the exception of ________, all the senses are fully developed and functioning at birth. Newborns prefer ________ -pitched sounds, ________ objects, and the taste of ________ substances. The newborn is also capable of ________ from experience. There is evidence for some continuity between temperament and ________ patterns in infancy and in later life. (352)
faces voices	**18.** The baby's favorite sight and sound are human ________ and ________. (352)
ten age/weight 5 weight years physical learning IQ/middle expectations child abuse	**19.** One out of ________ babies in the United States is born prematurely. The chance that a premature infant will survive depends on its ________ and ________; an infant born at seven or eight months' gestation and weighing above ________ pounds has an excellent chance for survival. Environmental stimulation facilitates infant ________ gain. By the age of 2 ________, the premature infant seems to "catch up" to full-terms on most ________ abilities. But premature infants remain more susceptible to perceptual, motor, and ________ difficulties in later childhood, and score slightly lower on ________ tests in ________ childhood. However, this last finding may be due to lowered parental ________. Premature infants have been overrepresented in cases of ________. (356)

two-thirds
ten
anxieties

emotional

20. Postpartum blues occur in ________ of all new mothers within the first ________ days after the birth. The new father may also be particularly inclined at this time to have ________ about the ability to raise a child. Both parents may also fear that the child will have unpredictable effects on their own ________ relationship. (355)

PSYCHOLOGICAL ISSUE: *BIRTH ORDER*

less

football/first

recognition
unreliable/small

small
last

21. The people ________ likely to show pain tolerance, more likely to show notable intellectual achievement, and less likely to be notable ________ players are the ________-borns. Adler's explanation for their greater achievement is that they may have a greater need for ________. Many findings on birth order are ________, because they are based on ________ samples of people. There is support, however, for the findings that (1) people who grow up in ________ families tend to get higher scores on tests of intelligence, and (2) the ________ -borns tend to have the lowest IQ scores. (362)

intellectual
helpful
nurturant/socially
liked
independent or autonomous
do not

22. According to Zajonc, the presence of an older sibling dilutes the newborn's ________ environment. (362)

23. Children who have younger siblings tend to be more ________ and ________; later-borns are more ________ skilled and better ________. (363)

24. Only children seem to be especially ________, and ________ seem to be more lonely, selfish, or maladjusted. (363)

Self-Quiz

1. Blue eye color is least likely to involve or illustrate:
   a. DNA.
   b. genotype.
   c. phenotype.
   d. natural selection.

2. Which one of the following traits is not controlled by a single gene pair?
   a. Blood type.
   b. Color vision.
   c. Intelligence level.
   d. Hair color.

3. Which statement is least accurate of the relationship between genes and behavior?
   a. Genes affect the development of the brain and the nervous system.
   b. Genes affect the enzymes that help regulate our chemical processes.
   c. The gray rat is tamed more easily than the white rat.
   d. Genes don't produce behavior—people do.

4. Which statement is not true?
   a. Forty percent of infant deaths can be attributed to genetic disorders.
   b. Twins occurs every 190 births.
   c. Genetic disorders account for 80 percent of all cases of retardation.
   d. If the mother has rubella in the first trimester, the child may be harmed.

5. Children with phenylketonuria may display all but which one of the following?
   a. Mental retardation.
   b. Hyperactivity.
   c. Visual disorders and eye discoloration.
   d. Epileptic-like seizures.

6. Which statement is not true of genetically related diseases?
   a. Four percent to 5 percent of American blacks are carriers of the gene for sickle-cell anemia.
   b. One percent of American blacks suffer from sickle-cell anemia.
   c. Sickle-cell anemia is ultimately fatal.
   d. Cystic fibrosis afflicts only Northern European whites.

7. Which one of the following statements is not true of Down's syndrome?
   a. It is inherited from the parents.
   b. It can be detected by amniocentesis.
   c. It is more likely if the pregnant woman is over 40.
   d. Children with this condition have a flat face and slanted eyes.

8. Which one of the following was not named as a possible cause of adverse effects on an unborn child? The pregnant woman's:
   a. nutrition.
   b. use of tobacco.
   c. use of alcohol.
   d. blood pressure.

9. A woman may miss a menstrual period for all but which one of the following?
   a. Illness.
   b. Emotional disturbances.
   c. She wants to miss it.
   d. No apparent reason.

10. Which statement is not true of birth order?
   a. First-borns tend to tolerate more pain.
   b. First-borns tend to have higher IQs.
   c. First-borns tend to be less socially skilled.
   d. First-borns tend to be more helpful.

Answers: 1.d 2.c 3.c 4.b 5.c 6.a 7.a 8.d 9.c 10.a

Chapter 12

From Infancy to Adolescence

1. Why have psychologists devoted so much attention to infancy and childhood? (367)

THE NATURE OF DEVELOPMENT

2. Define development. Distinguish between maturation and learning. (367)

3. How have psychologists' views on the roles of maturation and learning changed? How does the example of language development illustrate the current view? (368)

4. Define critical periods and imprinting. Describe the studies by Lorenz and Scott. (370)

5. Describe the evidence for critical periods in humans. What conclusions do psychologists draw? (371)

INFANCY

6. List Piaget's four stages of cognitive development with the approximate ages. (372)

7. *BOX 1:* Describe the development of Piaget's approach and his research methods. (373)

8. Define sensorimotor period and describe the cognitive challenge faced by infants. (373)

9. Describe the principle of object permanence and describe the development of the concepts of causality, space, and time. (373)

10. Describe the development of attachment and stranger anxiety. (375)

11. Summarize Harlow's research with surrogate mothers. Contrast his conclusions with the secondary reinforcement interpretation of attachment. Define comfort contact. (375)

12. Summarize Erikson's view of the role of attachment and Ainsworth's research. Describe infant attachment to fathers. (376)

13. *BOX 2:* Summarize the negative views on day-care centers and Kagan's study. What do the authors conclude? (378)

CHILDHOOD

14. Define and specify the relationship between: (379)

    Preoperational period—

    Egocentrism—

    Nominal realism—

    Period of concrete operations—

    Conservation—

15. How do mistakes in problem solving show cognitive growth? What did Piaget call the "American question," and what is the answer to it? (380)

16. *BOX 3:* Summarize the Wallerstein/Kelly and Hetherington studies. What do studies of the long-term psychological effects of divorce on children show? (382)

17. Describe the authoritarian child-rearing style and three types of permissive child-rearing styles. What does the evidence suggest is the most effective style? (382)

18. Why are peer relations thought to be important? How do peer relations affect long-term development? List two ways psychologists help children with peer relations. (385)

ADOLESCENCE

19. What changes signal the beginning of adolescence? Describe the age variation for these changes. How is this variation related to self-consciousness? (386)

20. Describe the stage of formal operations. Is this stage universal? How is it related to self-consciousness? (386)

21. *BOX 4:* Identify Erikson. List two ways in which his theory differs from Freud's theory of development. (390)

22. *BOX 4:* List Erikson's eight stages, approximate ages, and how each psychosocial conflict can be resolved. (390)

(1)

(2)

(3)

(4)

(5)

(6)

(7)

(8)

23. Define identity formation. How is this need affected by the lower status of women? How do social movements fulfill this need? (389)

PSYCHOLOGICAL ISSUE: *EDUCATION*

24. Describe Summerhill. What are the effects of recent reforms in American education? (393)

25. Define self-fulfilling prophecy. Describe Rosenthal's study in the classroom. What conclusions can be drawn? (394)

26. Describe Head Start. How effective has it been? Why do psychologists remain optimistic? What is White's suggestion? (395)

27. What are the effects of recent children's TV programs? What are the Singers' conclusions? (396)

28. Describe Atkinson's applications of CAI. How does it compare to a teacher in individualizing instruction? (396)

Self-Quiz

1. The unfolding of inherited biological patterns that are "preprogrammed" into the individual is called:
   a. instinct.
   b. learning.
   c. modeling.
   d. maturation. (Study Question 2)

2. Psychologists now believe that critical periods:
   a. occur throughout the life cycle.

b. cannot occur in language development.
c. are not well supported by research with humans.
d. are limited to adolescence. (Study Question 5)

3. Object permanence is first evident during the:
a. sensorimotor period.
b. preoperational period.
c. concrete-operational period.
d. formal-operational period. (Study Question 9)

4. Stranger anxiety occurs:
a. in a child's third year.
b. primarily in children who have had no opportunity to become attached to a mothering figure.
c. in children who are most predisposed to disturbance later in life.
d. toward the end of a child's first year and disappears typically during the second year. (Study Question 10)

5. Harlow's research on infant Rhesus monkeys found that attachment to a caretaker is:
a. a learned response to food.
b. an innate response to food.
c. an innate tendency for contact comfort.
d. an offshoot of play behavior in infancy. (Study Question 11)

6. Conservation characterizes the:
a. sensorimotor period.
b. preoperational period.
c. concrete-operational period.
d. formal-operational period. (Study Question 14)

7. Baumrind found that the most creative and cooperative preschoolers had parents who:
a. had definite standards.
b. solicited the child's opinions.
c. encouraged the child's independence.
d. all of the above. (Study Question 17)

8. The wide variation in the age at which the growth spurt and sexual maturation occur:
a. corresponds to variations in cognitive development.
b. is a major cause of self-consciousness.
c. is partly the result of different styles of child rearing.
d. none of the above. (Study Question 19)

9. A resolution to the conflict over intimacy versus isolation is sought, according to Erikson, in:
a. the elementary-school-age child.
b. adolescence.
c. early adulthood.
d. middle age. (Study Question 22)

10. Evaluations of the Head Start program have shown:
   a. IQ gains which disappear within two years.
   b. IQ gains which do not appear for several years.
   c. Lasting gains in both IQ and social development.
   d. no long-term positive effects. (Study Question 26)

Answers to Self-Quiz: 1.d 2.c 3.a 4.d 5.c 6.c 7.d 8.b 9.c 10.a

Programmed Review Unit

Answers	
50	1. By the end of the second year the infant has a vocabulary of at least ________ words. (366)
	THE NATURE OF DEVELOPMENT
Development **older**	2. ________ refers to the enduring changes in people's capacities and behavior that occur as they grow ________. (367)
short-term **generalize**	3. Some capacities, like ________ memory, often decline as a person gets older, while other capacities, like the ability to ________, remain stable or even improve. (368)
without **physical** **motor** **under** **learning** **social** **interplay** **futile**	4. The process of maturation, unlike learning, refers to changes that take place ________ any specific experience; this process is particularly obvious in the areas of ________ and ________ development. Kagan (1976) believes that we tend to ________-estimate the role of maturation and overestimate the role of ________, particularly in cognitive and ________ development. One of the implications of the ________ of learning and maturation is that it may be ________ to try to teach something before a person is maturationally ready. (368)
Critical **imprint** **language** **irreversibility**	5. ________ periods are times when behaviors must be learned or they won't ever be learned. Ducklings will ________ on the first moving object they see after hatching. Lenneberg (1967) believes the critical period for humans to learn ________ begins around age 2. Kagan doubts the "doctrine of ________." (369)
sequences **ages**	6. Whereas the ________ of developmental milestones are relatively consistent across individuals, the specific ________ are not. (371)
	INFANCY
2/preoperational **7/concrete** **12/formal**	7. In Piaget's theory of cognitive development the sensorimotor period goes from birth to age ________, the ________ period goes to age ________, the ________-operational period goes until age ________, and the ________ -operational period goes from then on. (372)

motor
permanence
8/9
causality
space
8
15
attachment
contact
trust
cognitive
3
diapers

8. The infant's first cognitive challenge is to coordinate impressions gained through her or his senses with her or his ________________ activities, such as reaching for objects. During the first year of life infants are discovering the principle of object ________________. Also around the ages of ________________ or ________________ months infants develop basic conceptions of time, ________________, and ________________. (373)

9. Stranger anxiety reaches its peak at around ________________ months and generally disappears by ________________ months. (375)

10. Harlow (1959) believes that ________________ is not a learned response to a food-giving object, but rather an innate tendency to love ________________ comfort. In Erikson's scheme this is the time when the child is learning to feel ________________. (375)

11. Ainsworth (1967) found that "secure" infants perform better on ________________ tasks at age 2 and are more competent with peers at age ________________. The degree of the infant's attachment to the father was directly related to the number of ________________ he changed per week. (376)

CHILDHOOD

harmful
social
38
egocentrism
symbols
realism
mentally
mass
shape
accelerate
competence
third
loneliness/anger
blamed/most
creativity/ played
less
hostility
reliant
divorced

12. Well-managed day care is not ________________ to the child in developing intellectual or ________________ competence. In 1975, only ________________ percent of the day-care centers in the United States were rated as being of high quality. (378)

13. Piaget calls the child's inability to take another person's point of view ________________. At the beginning of the preoperational period, children sometimes confuse names and ________________ with the objects they stand for, a phenomenon called nominal ________________. (379)

14. In the concrete-operations period children can count ________________ and can conserve a substance's weight, ________________, or volume even if it changes in ________________. (379)

15. Elkind (1975) thinks there is no evidence that there are any long-term effects of outside efforts to ________________ a child's intellectual development. (380)

16. The extent to which children develop ________________ depends to a large extent on their parents' approach to child rearing. (382)

17. By 1990, one-________________ of children under 18 in the United States will have experienced the divorce of their parents. Children often felt sadness, ________________, and ________________, and often ________________ themselves. After one year ________________ of the children had learned to cope at least moderately well. Hetherington et al. (1978, 1979) found that preschoolers from divorced homes showed less ________________ and imagination, and ________________ less often with other children. Children from broken homes experience ________________ unhappiness in the long run than children in unbroken homes that are full of conflict and ________________, according to Bane (1979), and may also be more self-________________ and responsible (Weiss, 1979). Such children are more likely to become adults who get ________________. (382)

standards/independence
opinions
clearly
decisions

18. Baumrind (1971) concludes that the most independent, creative, and cooperative children are those whose parents have definite ________ but encourage their children's ________ and solicit their ________. Coopersmith (1967) found that boys were more likely to develop high self-esteem if their parents provided them with ________ defined limits, and respected the boys' right to make ________ within those limits. (383)

peers
psychiatric

19. Sullivan (1953) believes that children's relationships with ________ affect their long-term development. Cowen et al. (1973) found that ratings of 8-year-old children by their classmates were related to the likelihood of developing ________ difficulties over the next 11 to 13 years. (384)

ADOLESCENCE

13
assured
adulthood

20. The average age of menarche in American girls is about ________. Late-maturing boys may feel less adequate and self-________ and more anxious even in ________. (386)

possible
hypotheses/thought
universal
conscious

21. An adolescent can think about what is ________, as well as what is real, and can consider and test all solutions to problems and generate ________; they can think about ________. Piaget (1972) and others have speculated that, unlike the earlier stages of cognitive development, the stage of formal operation may not be ________. During this stage people learn to be self-________. (388)

identity
trust/mistrust
year/autonomy
doubt/second
third/initiative
guilt/4
5/industry
6
11
role confusion/12
18/intimacy
generativity
integrity/despair

22. Erikson would say the development of ________ is the central task of adolescence. Erikson's eight stages are: (1) the stage of ________ versus ________, which occurs in the first ________ of life; (2) the conflict between ________ and ________, which occurs in the ________ and ________ years; (3) the conflict between ________ versus ________, which occurs at ages ________ to ________; (4) the conflict between ________ versus inferiority, which occurs between the ages of ________ and ________; (5) the conflict between identity versus ________, which occurs between ________ and ________; (6) the conflict between ________ versus isolation in young adulthood; (7) the conflict between ________ versus self-absorption in middle adulthood, and (8) the conflict between ________ versus ________ in the remaining years. (390)

women
identity

23. Douvan and Adelson (1966) suggest that because of their lower status in American society, ________ find it harder to develop a stronger sense of ________, and often postpone this task until after marriage. (389)

PSYCHOLOGICAL ISSUE: *EDUCATION*

reading

24. The U.S. Department of HEW found a steady decline in students' ________ abilities between 1965 and 1975, and between 1963

verbal and 1975 SAT ________________ scores dropped. Rosenthal and
Jacobson (1968) found that, if teachers expected students to do well, the
intelligence students would do better on ________________ tests.
Long ________________-term effects of Project Head Start include less
likelihood of needing special classes or repetition of grades. Head Start
3 programs for ________________-year-olds have been found to yield
gains one and a half times greater than programs for 4-year-olds. Burton
8 months White believes that between ________________ and
18 months ________________ is an especially critical time for the development of
the child's full potential. Children who are regularly exposed to
Sesame Street ________________ may interact more positively with adults and make
inferences ________________, a basic part of problem solving. (394)

25. Atkinson (1974) found that computer-assisted instruction (CAI) of reading
helped third-graders get to an average reading grade level of
4.1 ________________, versus 2.9 for students who did not have CAI. The
individualizing biggest advantage of CAI is ________________ instruction. (396)

Self-Quiz

1. Which one of the following statements is not true of learning and maturation?

a. Maturation refers to changes that take place without being the result of any specific experience.
b. The impact of maturation is obvious in the areas of physical and motor development.
c. Kagan believes we overestimate the role of maturation.
d. Kagan believes we overestimate the role of learning in cognitive and social development.

2. A person is first able to conserve a substance's weight, mass, or volume despite its shape in the ________________ period of cognitive development.

a. concrete-operational
b. formal-operational
c. preoperational
d. sensorimotor

3. At around 8 or 9 months, on the average, infants develop all but which one of the following basic concepts?

a. Object constancy.
b. Density.
c. Causality.
d. Space.

4. The peak of stranger anxiety occurs, on the average, at around:

a. 4 months.
b. 6 months.
c. 8 months.
d. 15 months.

5. Harlow found that the most important variable in influencing the infant's attachment to objects is:
   a. whether the object is its mother.
   b. whether the object gives food.
   c. whether the object is familiar.
   d. whether the object gives contact comfort.

6. Erikson believes that the infant's first interactions will determine the outcome of the conflict of:
   a. autonomy versus despair.
   b. trust versus mistrust.
   c. intimacy versus isolation.
   d. identity versus role confusion.

7. Which one of the following statements is false?
   a. Children who watch *Sesame Street* interact more positively with adults.
   b. Most children of broken homes are coping poorly a year later.
   c. The biggest advantage of computer-assisted instruction is individualized instruction.
   d. Reading and verbal skills declined from 1965 to 1975.

8. Self-consciousness is associated with the ability to think about thought, which occurs in which of Piaget's stages of cognitive development?
   a. Concrete-operational.
   b. Formal-operational.
   c. Preoperational.
   d. Sensorimotor.

9. In late adulthood, according to Erikson, people are focusing on the theme of:
   a. intimacy.
   b. integrity.
   c. generativity.
   d. identity.

10. Which statement is not true?
   a. Older people may show declines in short-term memory.
   b. The formal operations stage is universal.
   c. Computer-assisted instruction improves reading scores.
   d. The average age of menarche in American girls is around 13.

Answers: 1.c 2.a 3.b 4.c 5.d 6.b 7.b 8.b 9.b 10.b

Chapter 13

Adulthood and Aging

THE NATURE OF ADULT DEVELOPMENT

1. Distinguish age-graded and non-age-graded influences on development. How does the influence of each vary through the life cycle? (400)

2. Describe the central psychological challenges of early, middle, and late adulthood according to Erikson. (401)

3. Define longitudinal study. How does it answer questions of stability versus change in adult development? From such studies what remains relatively stable and what changes in adulthood? (401)

4. *BOX 1:* Summarize the overall findings of the Bengtson study. How are generational differences explained? Define cohort effect. (403)

EARLY ADULTHOOD

5. List the physical and cognitive changes in early adulthood. What are the most significant changes in this period? (402)

6. Define: (404)

   Life structure—

   Early Adult Transition—

   Entering the Adult World—

   Age 20 Transition—

   Settling Down—

7. What is Levinson's view on stages of adult development? How do other researchers disagree with him? (405)

8. Describe early career decisions and the effects of reality shock. Distinguish between external and internal career path. (406)

9. According to Erikson, what is the relationship between identity and intimacy in early adulthood? What does recent research show? (407)

10. How does having children affect parents? How does family timing point up the tasks of early adulthood? Define voluntary childlessness. (408)

MIDDLE ADULTHOOD

11. List all the physical changes that occur in middle adulthood and factors that make some of them more or less troublesome. (410)

12. *BOX 2:* Define menopause and climacteric. What is the effect of menopause on female development? (412)

13. Summarize Levinson's ideas of midlife transition and midlife crisis. What is controversial about these ideas? (413)

14. *BOX 3:* What do the Ochs and Strode cases illustrate about midlife transition? (414)

15. Summarize personality changes in middle adulthood, and list the various ways of achieving generativity. (416)

LATE ADULTHOOD

16. List the physical changes that occur in late adulthood. Describe the two theories of aging that examine individual cells. (417)

17. Describe theories of aging based on the immune system and the endocrine system. Describe senile dementia. (419)

18. *BOX 4:* Describe ageism and individual differences in old age. Describe two sources of ageism and tell why it might be expected to decline. (418)

19. Distinguish between fluid and crystallized intelligence. How do these change with age? (420)

20. Distinguish between cross-sectional and longitudinal studies. How does the distinction invalidate early studies of intelligence and age? What does Hebb's experience illustrate? (420)

21. What determines satisfaction in retirement? What three factors did Stevens-Long find? (421)

22. List the facts about widowhood. (423)

23. Summarize the late adult's relationship with adult children and friends. What are the primary reasons for institutionalization; what is the recent trend? (424)

24. Describe these three views of successful aging: (425)

Disengagement theory—

Neugarten's view—

Erikson's view—

25. Define life review and describe the functions of this process. (426)

PSYCHOLOGICAL ISSUE: *FACING DEATH*

26. How is denial of death exhibited? Describe the five stages of dying identified by Kubler-Ross. (429)

27. Summarize the results of the Kalish and Reynolds study. List Schultz's three major needs of dying persons. Define hospice. (431)

28. List the 1968 criteria for death. Describe the results of Ring's study. What controversies surround these findings? (433)

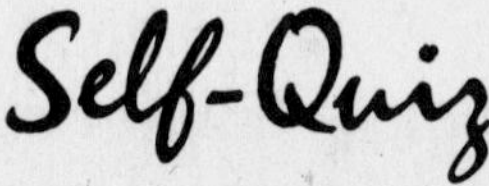

1. According to Erikson, the central psychological challenge of early adulthood is:
a. career stability.
b. an intimate relationship.
c. personal integrity.
d. freedom from parental authority. (Study Question 2)

2. Cohort effects refer to:
a. differences based on historical changes.
b. the effects of peer groups on attitudes.
c. changes that occur as a result of maturation.
d. the tendency of individuals to become more conservative with age. (Study Question 4)

3. Levinson's Early Adult Transition stage:
a. follows adolescence.
b. involves creating a stable life structure.
c. is the period in which families and careers are begun.
d. makes one a full-fledged senior member of the adult world. (Study Question 6)

4. The decision to remain childfree:
a. is usually made before marriage.
b. is usually made early in marriage.
c. usually occurs after a diagnosis of infertility.
d. is usually an extension of continual postponements. (Study Question 10)

5. According to research, the postmenopause, nonfertile woman:
   a. enjoys sex less.
   b. goes through a brief period of depression before she adjusts.
   c. enjoys sex more than ever.
   d. fears reentry into the job market. (Study Question 12)

6. The opportunity to become a mentor in middle age is a way of achieving:
   a. generativity.
   b. integrity.
   c. productivity.
   d. intimacy. (Study Question 15)

7. Negative attitudes toward aging may decline because:
   a. old people represent a larger portion of the population.
   b. older people are remaining more physically active.
   c. older people are now more physically attractive.
   d. old people behave like they did when they were younger. (Study Question 18)

8. The major milestone of late adulthood is:
   a. widowhood.
   b. grandchildren.
   c. physical disability.
   d. retirement. (Study Question 21)

9. The disengagement theory suggests the best way to age is to:
   a. select a way which is most appropriate to the individual.
   b. gradually withdraw from society.
   c. establish ego integrity.
   d. proceed with a life review. (Study Question 24)

10. Kalish and Reynolds found the age group least likely to fear death was:
   a. 11 – 19.
   b. 20 – 39.
   c. 40 – 59.
   d. over 60. (Study Question 27)

Answers to Self-Quiz: 1.b 2.a 3.a 4.d 5.c 6.a 7.a 8.d 9.b 10.d

Programmed Review Unit

THE NATURE OF ADULT DEVELOPMENT

maturational
experience

1. When a woman will have her menopause and whether and when a man will bald are changes that are primarily ________________, which are less influential than changes due to ________________. (399)

individual

2. Non-age-graded influences are experiences that are unique to the ________________ rather than associated with a particular stage of life.

infancy and childhood	Age-graded influences are especially common in ________.
social	There is greater diversity of ________ paths in adulthood. (400)
intimacy	3. In early childhood, Erikson believes the central challenge is to establish ________, while in middle adulthood the central challenge is
generation	to have an impact on the next ________, and in late adulthood the central theme is being able to look back at one's life with
satisfaction	________. (401)
stability/change	4. A central issue in the study of adult development is the degree to which a person shows ________ versus ________. The best way to answer questions about changes in adult's development is through
longitudinal	________ studies. Haan and Day (1974) found people who are
energetic and active	________ in their youth that way in late adulthood. The
outgoingness	personal trait of ________ also appears to be stable. (401)

EARLY ADULTHOOD

greater	5. Bengtson (1973) found that grandparents assign ________ importance to religious participation, describe themselves as much more
conservative	________ politically, and appear to be more
happy	________ than young people. The people most interested in
middle-aged	achievement are the ________. Generational differences based on historical change rather than processes of individual development are
cohort	called ________ effects. (403)
twenties/reaction	6. Physical strength and heart functions peak in the mid-________, as do sensory activity and ________ time. (402)
transition/22	7. Levinson (1978) believes that men in young adulthood go through the stages of (1) early adulthood ________ (ages 17 –), (2)
28	entering the adult world (ages 22 –________), (3) the age 30
settling down	transition (ages 28 –33), and (4) ________ (ages 33 –40). Other
continuous	researchers prefer to view life in terms of ________ movement rather than stages. Other researchers question whether Levinson's theory
women	applies to ________. (404)
external	8. The ________ career path is the job that the person occupies,
perceptions	while the internal career path is the self-________ that orient a person's occupational life. (406)
identity	9. Men and women who had achieved a clear sense of ________ were found to have deeper and more committed relationships; each of these developments could influence the other. (407)
20	10. One out of every ________ married couples do not have any children. Parents typically report that having children makes them feel
adult	more like an ________, but report spending
less time	________ ________ together. Couples who had children later reported that the postponement solidified the
marriage/careers	________ but created conflicts with ________. (408)

MIDDLE ADULTHOOD

gradual	11. Physical changes from 40 to 65 are generally ________. More
reacts	important than the changes is how the person ________. The

heart	risk of ________ disease, which is the primary cause of death for men in the United States, is highest between 50 and
60	________. The risk of breast cancer for women is greatest in
middle	________ age. One's susceptibility to disease is increased by
stress/tobacco	________ in the job or family, ________ or
alcohol/exercise	________ abuse, overeating, and lack of ________.
sexual	Changes in ________ functioning also occur in middle age, as does speed of copying numbers. The extent of change is largely
physical	determined by individual ________ condition,
attitudes/habits	________, and ________. Exercise programs begun
do	late in life ________ yield improvements in physical capacity.
need not	The woman's menopause ________ interfere with her sexual functioning. (411)
two years	**12.** Menopause typically lasts ________ and occurs around 45 to
50	________. The climacteric is a process of physical and sexual
slowing down	________. (412)
more	**13.** Middle-aged workers benefited ________ than younger workers from increased lighting. (412)
80	**14.** Levinson found that ________ percent of the men he studied had a painful and disruptive struggle in the midlife transition, which
40/five	began around age ________ and lasted ________
time	years. Midlife may bring on a new ________ orientation. Levinson's formulation of the midlife transition is highly
controversial/larger	________; statistical studies with ________ samples have generally failed to suport his conclusion that personal turmoil are at their height between 40 and 45. (415)
	15. Evidence shows that middle adulthood is associated with increasing
knowledge/sex-role	self-________; this may include ________ reversal. (415)
	16. One of the most important career rewards of many middle-aged people is
mentor	the opportunity to be a ________. (416)

LATE ADULTHOOD

twice	**17.** The age group of people 65 and over grew ________ as fast as the U.S. population as a whole between 1953 and 1978, and in 1980 made
10	up ________ percent of the U.S. population. (416)
	18. Many physical changes become more marked in the late
sixties	________. (417)
reproducing	**19.** Cells eventually stop ________ themselves. In old age the
immune	________ system may become disorganized, as may the
endocrine	________ system. (417)
brain	**20.** Senility is due to damage to ________ cells, and may be
memory	reflected by loss of ________, disorientation in
time/place	________ and ________, impaired
attention	________, and loss of ability to acquire new
information/minority	________. Senility afflicts a ________ of
very	________ old people. Its symptoms are sometimes mistaken
cured	for those of other diseases that can be ________. (419)
increase	**21.** Intelligence may ________ well into the seventies. Fluid

nonverbal
education
central nervous
more
Crystallized
eighties
cross-sectional

intelligence is mental agility, especially ________ skills, that allows people to see old problems in new ways. Crystallized intelligence includes verbal skills and other information accumulated through living in society, including formal ________. Fluid intelligence is thought to be more sensitive to changes in the ________ system, and is ________ likely to decline over time; ________ intelligence appears to remain the same or improve at least until the early ________. Earlier studies showed intelligence declines because they used the ________ approach rather than longitudinal designs. (420)

discrimination
more/less
discomfort

22. Ageism is ________ against old people. Older people tend to be ________ cautious and ________ flexible. Ageism reflects the ________ that young people have with older adults. (418)

14
health
income
leisure
time

23. The average worker spends ________ years in retirement, which is satisfying as long as people have good ________ and adequate ________. Stevens-Long (1979) suggests that people can become comfortable with a ________-centered life if they have enough money, learn to value leisure, and learn to use their ________ in a new way. (421)

sixties
more
lonelier
less

24. More than half of married women in the United States are widowed by their early ________. People who have been single throughout their lives felt ________ satisfied in late adulthood than did widows and widowers. Widowers felt ________ and ________ happy than widows. (423)

80
12
independence/Half
continue
reduced
loneliness

25. Although ________ percent of older people in the United States have living children, only ________ percent of them live with a grown child; one reason is a mutual wish for ________ and privacy. ________ of the older persons saw a grown child frequently. People who have few friends or many friends when younger tend to ________ their pattern of sociability when older. Social contacts are ________ as we grow older. Friends play a larger role than relatives in preventing ________. (423)

4/5

26. Only ________ to ________ percent of the aged population are currently institutionalized. (424)

satisfied

27. Disengagement theory is not supported by studies of which elderly are the most ________—they tend to be socially active and involved with their families and communities. (425)

successfully
integrity
review

28. Neugarten (1972) stresses that there are many ways to age ________. Erikson (1950) believes that the major developmental task of the old is to establish ego ________, which may be established by what Butler calls the life ________. (426)

PSYCHOLOGICAL ISSUE: *FACING DEATH*

cancer
strokes
accidents

29. The leading causes of death are heart disease, ________, and ________. The most common cause of death for people between 25 and 34 is ________. Kubler-Ross (1969) believes

	the five stages that dying persons experience are (in order):
denial/anger	________, ________, bargaining,
depression/acceptance	________, and ________. Older people think
more/less	________ about death and are ________ frightened by it. Schultz believes the three major needs of dying persons are relief
pain/worth	from ________, a sense of self-________, and
love/60	________ and affection. Over ________ percent of us die in hospitals and nursing homes. One of the major goals of the
isolation	hospice movement is to break down the ________ that usually surrounds a dying person. Riney (1980) found that 48 percent of the
recollection	patients who had come close to death had some ________ of the event. (431)

Self-Quiz

1. According to Erikson young adults are struggling with the crisis of:
- **a.** trust versus mistrust.
- **b.** identity versus role confusion.
- **c.** intimacy versus isolation.
- **d.** ego integrity versus despair.

2. The leading cause of death in people aged 25 – 34 is:
- **a.** heart disease.
- **b.** cancer.
- **c.** strokes.
- **d.** accidents.

3. Bengtson found that the happiest people are:
- **a.** children.
- **b.** parents.
- **c.** grandparents.
- **d.** none of the above.

4. Crystallized intelligence is characterized by all but which one of the following?
- **a.** It is accumulated through formal education.
- **b.** It declines with age.
- **c.** It is more verbal than fluid intelligence.
- **d.** It is less sensitive than fluid intelligence to changes in the central nervous system.

5. Which statement is false?
- **a.** There is less diversity in people as they get older.
- **b.** Longitudinal studies are better than cross-sectional studies for answering questions about how people change.
- **c.** The personality trait of outgoingness appears to be stable.
- **d.** The characteristic of activity level appears to be stable.

6. The mid-twenties are the peak for all but which one of the following?
   a. Physical strength.
   b. The climacteric.
   c. Sensory acuity.
   d. Reaction time.

7. Levinson's theory is characterized by all but which one of the following?
   a. It describes stages of growth.
   b. It is based on 40 males.
   c. It states that it is likely that a person aged 40 – 45 will experience turmoil.
   d. It is generally accepted by psychologists.

8. Which statement is false regarding parenthood?
   a. One married couple in 100 does not have children.
   b. Couples with children spend less time together.
   c. Couples felt that having children made them feel more adult.
   d. Couples felt that postponement fo children solidified their marriage.

9. One's susceptibility to disease is related to all but which one of the following?
   a. Stress in one's job or family.
   b. Abuse of tobacco or alcohol.
   c. Overeating.
   d. Too much sex.

10. Which one of the following statements is false?
    a. Senility affects a majority of the very old.
    b. The average worker spends 14 years in retirement.
    c. Widowers felt lonelier than widows.
    d. Only 4 to 5 percent of the aged population are currently institutionalized.

Answers: 1.c 2.d 3.c 4.b 5.a 6.b 7.d 8.a 9.d 10.a

Chapter 14

The Nature of Abnormality

THE HISTORY OF ABNORMALITY

1. What two views have dominated the history of abnormality? Describe the approach to mental disorder in the early Greek and Roman eras. (436)

2. Identify Hippocrates and his contribution to the scientific approach to mental disorder. What Romans carried on this tradition? (438)

3. Contrast the treatment of the mentally ill in the early and late Middle Ages. Identify Pope Innocent VII and *The Witch's Hammer*. What were mental institutions like in the late Middle Ages? (440)

4. Identify the following and their contributions: (440)

Pinel—

Esquirol—

Tuke—

Dix—

Beers—

DEFINING ABNORMALITY

5. Describe the statistical approach to defining abnormality. What are its limitations? (441)

6. What are the two elements in the *DSM-III* definition of abnormality? What are the problems with the adequacy approach? (442)

THE MEDICAL MODEL

7. How is the medical model of abnormality rooted in organic disorder? What is the evidence for the persistence of this model? (442)

8. List three arguments of those who favor the medical model. (443)

9. Identify Szasz. Describe the arguments against the medical model. How do psychiatrists and psychologists differ on this issue? (443)

10. *BOX 1:* Distinguish among these definitions of insanity: (444)

M'Naghten rule—

Durham rule—

American Law Institute—

11. *BOX 1:* List the current controversies about the legal concept of insanity. (445)

12. Define cultural model of abnormality. How does the example of homosexuality illustrate this model? (444)

13. Cite examples of how the same behavior may be either normal or abnormal depending on the context. Summarize Broverman's findings. (446)

THE PROBLEM OF CLASSIFICATION

14. Distinguish between diagnosis and explanation. Summarize the data on the reliability of diagnostic judgments. Define reliability. (447)

15. How does the *DSM-III* address the reasons for unreliable diagnostic judgments? Define validity. How is it related to reliability? (448)

16. *BOX 2:* Define *DSM-III*. List three major controversies surrounding the development of *DSM-III*. (449)

17. Describe the Langer and Abelson study. What does it illustrate and what are its implications? (450)

18. *BOX 3:* Describe the method of Rosenhan's study. (451)

19. *BOX 3:* List the results of Rosenhan's study. What criticism was made of his conclusions? (451)

THE PREVALENCE OF DISORDER

20. Distinguish among three views (medical model, antimedical model, and Freudian) on the prevalence of disorder. What is Gross' position? (452)

PSYCHOLOGICAL ISSUE: *ALCOHOLISM*

21. How does alcohol alter one's psychological state? List the steps to alcoholism. What are the negative effects of the derelict stereotype of alcoholics? (455)

22. Contrast the biological and psychodynamic theories of alcoholism. Summarize Jones' longitudinal study and the social influences in determining alcoholism. (457)

23. Why do many approaches to treating alcoholism involve the spouse? List the four principles of AA. What statistics back up the effectiveness of AA? (458)

24. Where do psychotherapists part company with AA? What is controlled drinking? What is the evidence for its effectiveness? (459)

Self-Quiz

1. The medical approach to mental disturbances:
   a. did not evolve until the mid-nineteenth century.
   b. existed in Ancient Greece.
   c. was spelled out in *Malleus Maleficarum.*
   d. was not adopted until Freud. (Study Question 1)

2. Starting in the Late Middle Ages, a deviant was often views as:
   a. having something physically wrong with his brain.
   b. a child of God.
   c. a witch.
   d. a person who had a hard, unfortunate life. (Study Question 3)

3. Homosexuality is most clearly abnormal if you use which definition of abnormality?
   a. Statistical.
   b. Adequacy.
   c. Medical.
   d. Cultural. (Study Questions 5, 6, 7, and 12)

4. The acceptance of the medical model:
   a. helped reform asylums.
   b. continues to the present day.
   c. persisted when it was apparent that many abnormal individuals had no physical disorder.
   d. all of the above. (Study Question 7)

5. The M'Naghten rule of legal insanity specified that a person was not criminally responsible if the person was:
   a. unable to distinguish right from wrong.
   b. suffering from a mental disease.
   c. unable to control his or her behavior.
   d. declared insane by two psychiatrists. (Study Question 10)

6. The cultural model of abnormality best accounts for the fact that:
   a. clinical psychologists have the same standard of mental health for both male and female Americans.
   b. homosexuality has always been considered an acceptable deviation.
   c. abnormality of a behavior depends on context.
   d. very rare behaviors are labeled abnormal. (Study Question 12)

7. The diagnosis of a particular behavior:
   a. gives an explanation of it.
   b. describes all the symptoms.
   c. is not likely to be agreed upon by psychologists to any great extent.
   d. all of the above. (Study Question 14)

8. Langer and Abelson showed a videotape of an interview to psychoanalytically oriented therapists and told half the therapists that

the man interviewed was a job applicant and the other half that he was a patient. They found that:

a. the therapists told they were viewing a patient rated the man in a much more negative way.

b. the therapists told that they were viewing a job applicant rated the man in a much more negative way.

c. the therapists evaluated the man similarly whether they had been told he was a patient or a job applicant.

d. the ratings varied considerably, but did not seem to be related to whether the therapists had been told the man was a patient or a job applicant. (Study Question 17)

9. Rosenhan's study "On being sane in insane places" found:

a. the pseudopatients were always detected.

b. the length of hospitalization never exceeded seven days.

c. other patients were aware of the normalcy of the pseudopatients.

d. pseudopatients were not administered drugs. (Study Question 19)

10. Most researchers agree that the most important causes of alcoholism are:

a. biological and unconscious factors.

b. psychological and social factors.

c. unconscious and social factors.

d. biological and social factors. (Study Question 22)

Answers to Self-Quiz: 1.b 2.c 3.a 4.d 5.a 6.c 7.c 8.a 9.c 10.b

Programmed Review Unit

illness / **physical** / **illness** / **judging**

1. One approach to abnormal behavior is to equate abnormality with psychopathology or mental ________—to say that psychological disturbances are not unlike ________ diseases. However, many psychologists maintain that abnormal behavior does not necessarily involve any "________," and may depend on who is doing the ________. (436)

THE HISTORY OF ABNORMALITY

medical / **religious**

2. In the Grecian era of Hippocrates, as well as today, a scientific or ________ view of psychological abnormality was dominant, while at other times the dominant view was a ________ perspective. (438)

chains / **statistical** / **hygiene** / **medical** / **biochemical**

3. Pinel revolutionized mental health care in Paris by freeing his patients from ________ and instituting more humane methods of treatment. Esquirol became one of the first to apply ________ methods to the study of patients. Beers created a public storm and launched the mental ________ movement to educate people in the understanding of mental problems. Today, ________ and ________ advances have stimulated new progress in the diagnosis and treatment of mental disorders. (440)

DEFINING ABNORMALITY

Answers	Item
statistical **geniuses** **conformity** **anxiety/depression** **little**	**4.** According to the ____ approach, any deviation from the majority would be abnormal. This would include ____, as well as the mentally retarded. A statistical definition suggests equating mental health with ____. And disorders like ____ or ____ are so common that from this viewpoint they are not abnormal; a purely statistical approach is of ____ value. (441)
environment **discomfort** **DSM-III**	**5.** The adequacy approach assesses how well people adjust to their ____. Adequacy can be judged in terms of the amount of ____ a person feels in everyday experiences, and appears in the definition of mental disorder presented in the book abbreviated ____. (442)

THE MEDICAL MODEL

Answers	Item
organic **myth** **external** **responsibility** **sick**	**6.** Many people who deviated from socially acceptable behavior do not have any ____ impairment. Szasz (1970) claims that mental illness is a ____. By assigning the causes of problems to some ____ force like illness, mental health professionals inadvertently encourage the individual to not take any ____ for his actions. The medical model may encourage people to view themselves as "____." (443)
sane/insane	**7.** It is difficult to determine whether a person is legally ____ or ____. (444)
norms **time** **homosexuality** **regularly/emotional** **generalized** **social**	**8.** According to the cultural model, your actions will be labeled abnormal if you behave in a way that does not follow the ____ of society, which change from one culture to another and one ____ to another, as shown in the example of ____. According to the Board of the American Psychiatric Association, "For a mental condition to be considered a psychiatric disorder, it should either ____ cause ____ distress or regularly be associated with ____ impairment of ____ functioning." (444)
situation/sex	**9.** The same behavior may be viewed as normal or abnormal depending on the ____ or the ____ of the person being assessed. (446)

THE PROBLEM OF CLASSIFICATION

Answers	Item
explanation **communicate/agreed-upon** **small** **reliability** **low/clear** **observable/interpretations** **higher**	**10.** A diagnostic label is merely a name and not an ____ of a behavior. Diagnostic categories can be useful in allowing psychologists to ____, ideally in an ____ manner about abnormal behavior. But Zigler and Phillips (1961) found that the relationship between individual symptoms and a particular category is quite ____. And Ullman and Krasner (1975) found that the ____ (extent of agreement) between experts about diagnostic classifications, though better than chance, is disturbingly ____, primarily because of a lack of ____ criteria. *DSM-III* uses clearer criteria, and now makes diagnoses based more on ____ symptoms than ____ of those symptoms. The use of clearer criteria has led to ____ reliability. (448)

validity
cure
reliability

11. The ________________ of diagnoses relates to whether we can have an accurate understanding of the causes, can predict the course of the disorder, or "________________" the disorder. Without ________________ there cannot be much validity. (448)

internal
observable
neuroses

12. Psychoanalytic theory says disorder is the ________________ state of mind and not the ________________ symptom pattern; such theorists were bothered by *DSM-III*'s relabeling ________________ *anxiety disorders*. (449)

behavior
image
patient

13. A label also tends to produce the ________________ it represents and to alter the person's self-________________. Langer and Abelson (1974) showed how the label "________________" can by itself prime therapists to see more maladjustment. (450)

normally
never
19
schizophrenics/common

14. Despite the fact that Rosenhan's pseudopatients behaved ________________ once inside mental hospitals, they were ________________ detected. Length of hospitalization averaged ________________ days, and they were all labeled as ________________. It was ________________ for other patients to detect that a pseudopatient was not really one of them. (451)

THE PREVALENCE OF DISORDER

five
one-fourth
emotional

15. During World War II nearly one out of ________________ men were rejected for military service because of "mental illness." In 1978, the President's Commission on Mental Health estimated as many as ________________ of all Americans suffer at least mild to moderate depression, anxiety, or other indication of ________________ disorder. (452)

PSYCHOLOGICAL ISSUE: *ALCOHOLISM*

10
half/Seven
20
depressant
perceptions
forget
eaten

16. Alcohol misuse has been a factor in more than ________________ percent of all deaths in the United States, and more particularly, ________________ of all traffic deaths. ________________ percent of all Americans 18 or over are estimated to be problem drinkers; this is true of ________________ percent of the 14–17-year-olds. Alcohol is a ________________ that reduces the efficiency of many bodily systems, including sensations and ________________. You will get drunk quicker when you are celebrating than when you are trying to ________________, and alcohol's effects are quicker if you haven't ________________. (454)

5
recover
admit
psychological

17. Fewer than ________________ percent of alcoholics are "winos." About two-thirds of alcoholics who seek treatment ________________. The first problem is often to get problem drinkers to ________________ their problem. Most researchers agree that the most important causes of alcoholism are ________________ and social, not biological. (455)

oral
inferiority
destroy
are not

18. Freud viewed drinking as a sign of fixation at the ________________ stage of psychosexual development, Adler suggested it was caused by feelings of ________________, and Menninger felt it reflected a person's unconscious desire to ________________ himself. These theories ________________ supported by systematic evidence. (456)

parents
more/10
3

19. People learn to drink as their ________________ do. Drinking problems are ________________ common these days. About ________________ percent of adult males and ________________ percent of adult females

are currently problem drinkers or alcoholics. There are

many ________ reasons for drinking. (457)

spouse 20. Involving the ________ in treatment significantly increases the likelihood of positive outcome. (458)

21. The basic principles of Alcoholics Anonymous are that only an

alcoholic ________ can help an alcoholic, that psychiatric and other

unsuccessful treatment is usually ________, that alcoholics can manage to

normal lead ________ lives by banding together, and most

drink importantly, that an alcoholic must never again ________. AA members assert there is nothing wrong with alcoholics except

alcohol/physical ________ and that alcoholism is a ________ disease, not a mental one. Psychotherapists part company with the AA program when it states that the drug is a *cause* rather than a

symptom ________ of deeper problems. (458)

70 22. The Sobells (1973) found that ________ percent of the subjects who had learned controlled drinking were not drinking or drinking

35 moderately, compared to ________ percent of the group that received conventional treatments such as AA and group therapy. The Sobells taught controlled drinking habits through behavior therapy

role techniques, such as discussion, ________-playing, and

videotaped assertiveness training. Also, participants were ________ while

abstinence drunk. For some alcoholics, the total ________ advocated by AA may be the only way to maintain control over a drinking problem. (459)

Self-Quiz

1. Which one of the following statements is true of the prevalence of mental disorder?
   a. On any given day, 750,000 people are under psychiatric care in hospitals.
   b. One-eighth of all Americans suffer at least mild emotional disorder.
   c. Psychological disorder is not seen as highly prevalent in the United States.
   d. The statistical definition would suggest a greater number of abnormal people than would the adequacy approach.

2. Which one of the following statements is not true of alcoholism?
   a. Twenty-five percent of alcoholics are winos.
   b. The typical alcoholic is a male.
   c. Two-thirds of alcoholics who seek treatment recover.
   d. Freud's theory of alcoholism is not supported by research evidence.

3. Which one of the following is not characteristic of alcoholics?
   a. They can be taught to drink alcohol in a controlled manner.
   b. The likelihood of successful therapeutic outcome is significantly increased if the spouse is involved.
   c. AA believes that alcoholics can be taught to drink again.
   d. Assertiveness training teaches people how to successfully refuse a drink.

4. All but which one of the following was found in Rosenhan's study?
   a. The pseudopatients behaved normally once inside the mental hospital.
   b. The length of hospitalization averaged 19 days.
   c. They were eventually detected by the staff.
   d. They were frequently detected by the other patients.

5. Which one of the following is not true of the approaches to abnormality?
   a. According to the statistical approach geniuses are abnormal.
   b. The statistical approach suggests equating mental health with conformity.
   c. The statistical approach compares performance with capability.
   d. The adequacy approach examines the extent of personal discomfort.

6. Which one of the following is not true of the approaches to abnormality?
   a. A major problem with the adequacy approach is that "adequate" depends on the theoretical orientation of the judge.
   b. The cultural approach examines the deviation from social norms.
   c. Social norms are consistent across cultures.
   d. The American Psychiatric Association recently decided homosexuality was not a disorder.

7. Which one of the following is not true?
   a. Clinicians have different standards of mental health for males and females.
   b. The label of patient primes therapists to see maladjustment.
   c. Homosexuality is currently considered a disorder.
   d. *DSM-III* has more clear labels of disorders.

8. Which one of the following statements is not true of diagnostic categories?
   a. Ideally, they allow psychologists to communicate in an agreed-upon manner.
   b. The relationship between an individual's symptoms and the category into which she or he is placed is quite good.
   c. The reliability between classifications made by different experts on the same patients is low.
   d. A label tends to produce the behavior it represents.

9. Which statement is not true?
   a. Szasz believes mental illness is a myth.
   b. It is easy to legally determine if a person is insane.
   c. Without reliability there cannot be much validity.
   d. During World War II one in five men were rejected for military service because of mental illness.

10. Which one of the following statements is not true of alcoholism?
   a. In small amounts it is a depressant, not a stimulant.
   b. Alcohol accounts for half of U.S. highway deaths.
   c. Ten percent of American males are alcoholics.
   d. AA asserts that alcoholism is a mental disease, not a physical one.

Answers: 1.c 2.a 3.c 4.c 5.c 6.c 7.c 8.b 9.b 10.d

Chapter 15

Psychological Disorder

THE RANGE OF DISORDERS

1. Distinguish between neuroses (anxiety disorders) and psychoses. Define delusions and hallucination. (462)

2. *BOX 1:* Define: (463)

   Dissociative disorder—

   Amnesia—

   Fugue states—

   Multiple personality—

3. *BOX 1:* Summarize the cases of the *Three Faces of Eve* and *Sybil:* (463)

ANXIETY DISORDERS

4. Distinguish between anxiety and fear. Describe what is meant by anxiety attacks. (464)

5. Define: (465)

Phobia—

Agoraphobia—

Claustrophobia—

Acrophobia—

6. Describe the case of Little Hans and the psychoanalytic and behavioral interpretations of it. (467)

7. Identify Little Albert. What are the limitations of the behavioral approach to phobia and the evidence concerning individual differences? (467)

8. Describe obsessive-compulsive disorders and distinguish obsession from compulsion. What is the role of reaction formation? (468)

9. *BOX 2:* Define personality disorder, paranoid personality disorder, and schizoid personality disorder. Define antisocial personality disorder, giving its biological and social bases. (468)

DEPRESSION

10. Describe depression. How common is depression and how does it respond to treatment? (470)

11. *BOX 3:* How common is depression in college students? List five causes. Describe cognitive distortion and how it can be overcome. (471)

12. List the common symptoms of depression. Do all depressions have external causes? Define mania and bipolar disorders. (472)

13. Give the psychoanalytic explanation of depression. (473)

14. Describe Seligman's concept of learned helplessness. What are the implications for depression, especially in women? (473)

15. Describe the physiological factors in depression and bipolar disorders. (474)

SCHIZOPHRENIA

16. How common is schizophrenia in America and American mental institutions? List the hallmarks of schizophrenia. (474)

17. Distinguish the following types of schizophrenia: (475)

Disorganized—

Catatonic—

Paranoid—

Undifferentiated—

18. Define and distinguish: (475)

Delusions—

Delusions of persecution—

Ideas of reference—

Delusions of grandeur—

19. Define neologisms, loose associations, and clang associations. How is thought disorder related to schizophrenia? What difficulty is at the heart of schizophrenic disorder? (476)

20. Distinguish between reactive and process schizophrenia. What is the evidence for biological and genetic causes of schizophrenia? What is the likely biochemical mechanism? (476)

21. Summarize the roles of double-bind communication and psychological stress in schizophrenia. What is the current consensus among researchers about schizophrenia? (477)

22. *BOX 4:* Describe Laing's interpretation of schizophrenia. (479)

THE DISORDERS OF CHILDHOOD

23. Define and distinguish among the following terms: (479)

Conduct disorders—

Anxiety disorders—

"Childhood schizophrenia"—

Hyperactivity—

24. Describe the development of hyperactivity, its causes, and the controversy surrounding its treatment. (480)

25. Describe infantile autism, the autistic child's performance on intellectual tasks, and the development of autism. (480)

26. Contrast current ideas on the causes of autism with those of the recent past. What treatments are generally employed? How effective are they? (481)

PSYCHOLOGICAL ISSUE: *SUICIDE*

27. How common is suicide? Why are suicide statistics unreliable? What is the trend for suicide rates? (486)

28. Summarize the differences in suicide according to sex, age, marital status, and race. (487)

29. How is suicide related to psychological disorder? What is meant by the right to die? Describe what is being done to prevent suicide. (488)

1. The book *Sybil* concerns a classic case of:
a. dissociative disorder.
b. obsessive-compulsive dirorder.
c. paranoid schizophrenia.
d. bipolar disorder. (Study Question 3)

2. An excessive fear of heights is:
a. claustrophobia.
b. acrophobia.
c. agoraphobia.
d. locophobia. (Study Question 5)

3. John keeps thinking that while he is asleep he will somehow harm his son. He doesn't want to hurt his son, but keeps having thoughts that he might. To prevent this, every night he goes through an elaborate ritual of locking his son's bedroom door and putting chairs in front of it. This is an example of:
a. a dissociative reaction.
b. a phobia.
c. an anxiety attack.
d. obsessive-compulsive behavior. (Study Question 8)

4. Which of the following is not classified as a personality disorder?
a. Paranoid personality disorder.
b. Schizoid personality disorder.
c. Depressive personality disorder.
d. Antisocial personality disorder. (Study Question 9)

5. A physiological factor associated with depression is:
a. decrease in norepinephrine.
b. decrease in epinephrine.
c. increase in norepinephrine.
d. vitamin deficiency. (Study Question 15)

6. Which of the following is not true of schizophrenia and thought disorder?
a. About half the cases of schizophrenia have an associated thought disorder.
b. It is very difficult for schizophrenics to pick out relevant information.
c. Schizophrenics are distracted easily.
d. Schizophrenic thought disorder sometimes results in incoherent and rambling speech. (Study Question 19)

7. A mother's cold withdrawal from her son's affectionate hug followed by her statement that "you should not be so easily embarrassed and afraid of your feelings" is an example of:
   a. a dissociative reaction.
   b. double-bind communication.
   c. loose association.
   d. bizarre ideation. (Study Question 21)

8. Hyperactivity is what type of disorder?
   a. Affective.
   b. Neurotic
   c. Attention deficit.
   d. Autistic. (Study Question 23)

9. Which characteristic might be found in an autistic child?
   a. Excessive fear.
   b. Epileptic seizures.
   c. Manic behavior.
   d. Reluctance to be touched. (Study Question 25)

10. Research suggests that car accidents may often be:
   a. misplaced aggression.
   b. attempted suicides.
   c. sexually motivated.
   d. all of the above. (Study Question 27)

Answers to Self-Quiz: 1.a 2.b 3.d 4.c 5.a 6.a 7.b 8.c 9.d 10.b

Programmed Review Unit

DSM-III	1. This chapter uses the classification system presented in ________ to describe mental disorders. (460)

THE RANGE OF DISORDERS

fifteen **anxiety/depression** **schizophrenia/childhood** **personality** **personality**	2. The current classification system includes about ________ major categories of disorders. Four of the most common are: ________ disorders, ________, ________, and ________ disorders. The rare problem called multiple ________ is in the category of dissociative disorders, while antisocial personality disorder is in the category of ________ disorders. (461)
anxiety **social** **reality** **beliefs** **hallucinations**	3. Traditionally, there were two main groupings: neuroses are typically characterized by ________, an inability to cope effectively, and difficulty in ________ relationships; psychoses involve a loss of contact with ________, and may be demonstrated by delusions (false ________ about the person or her or his world), ________ (seeing or hearing things that aren't there),

feelings	disturbed thought processes, and loss of control over ________
actions	and ________. (461)
	4. Dissociative disorder occurs when a person unconsciously dissociates, or
removes	________, some part of his consciousness. These disorders
amnesia/fugue	include ________ and ________ states, in which the
location	person lives a new life in a different ________. (463)
Anxiety	**5.** ________ is the vague, unpleasant feeling that suggests that
	something bad is about to happen; fear is a reaction to something more
specific	________; anxiety and fear are quite similar. (464)
phobias	**6.** Anxiety disorders are frequently marked by ________
	intense fears of particular objects or activities that seem out of proportion
	to the real dangers involved. Phobias are most common in
childhood	________. According to the psychoanalytic view, phobias
repression	are symptoms of the ineffective ________ of unacceptable
learned	basic urges. The behavioral view is that phobias are ________.
	However, there are many reports of phobias that have developed without
experience/hereditary	the specific ________ and vice versa. A ________
	biological tendency to be susceptible to phobias may exist. (464)
master	**7.** The obsessive-compulsive person attempts to ________ a
	threat by repeatedly engaging in behavior connected with it, such as
ritualistic	thinking certain thoughts and engaging in ________ acts.
	Extreme neatness may also demonstrate the defense mechanism Freud
opposite	called reaction formation, where one does the ________ of the
	repressed desire or impulse. (468)
emotion	**8.** Charles Manson seemed to be without ________; he would
antisocial	probably be diagnosed as having an ________ personality
	disorder. A person with any of the personality disorders has a rigid and
responses	narrow range of ________ that restrict her or his way of
	relating to the environment. The paranoid personality disorder is
sensitivity	characterized by extreme ________ and general
suspiciousness	________, while people with a schizoid personality disorder
withdrawn or reclusive	tend to be ________. (468)
	9. There is some evidence that the antisocial personality disorder has a
biological	________ basis. These people are not anxious about the
outcome	________ of their behavior; the many jail sentences that
avoid	Manson served never taught him to ________ those actions
	that put him in jail. This disorder may be caused by lack of love and
discipline	________ in childhood, especially from one's
father	________. (468)

DEPRESSION

15	**10.** It has been estimated that about ________ percent of
	American adults have at some time had a major depression, which is
women	twice as common among ________. As many as
half	________ the suicides in the United States occur among
	persons suffering from depression. Depression is probably the most
susceptible	________ psychological disorder to effective
	treatment. (470)
one-fourth	**11.** At any one time ________ of all American college students are

three-fourths **distortion** **problems** **feedback**

suffering from symptoms of depression, and ________________ of all students suffer symptoms of depression at some time during each year of college. Beck and Young (1978) suggest that most students' depressions start because of cognitive ________________—exaggerating the importance of a particular problem. Students who confront their actual ________________ are better able to break out of the circle. To help get an objective perspective, ________________ from another person is helpful. (471)

mania/bipolar

12. When depression alternates with extreme elation, known as ________________, it is a ________________ disorder. (472)

dependent **self-esteem** **gratification/oral** **childhood** **helplessness** **outcome** **striving/mastery** **reinforcements** **actions**

13. Freud accounted for depression by suggesting that some people become excessively ________________ on others for the maintenance of their ________________, as a result of either too much or too little ________________ of their needs during the ________________ period of psychosexual development. Learning theorists agree that the predisposition to become seriously depressed may have roots in ________________ experience, but that it is the result of learned ________________—experience in which the person learns that his efforts have little to do with the ________________ of the situation. Depression may be avoided if children are encouraged to have experiences of active ________________ and ________________ in which they can see that positive and negative ________________ are contingent on their own ________________. (473)

norepinephrine/dopamine **serotonin/manic** **heritable** **lithium**

14. The physiological explanation of depression suggests the depletion of the neural transmitters ________________, ________________, and ________________, while the ________________ phase is associated with high levels of these transmitter substances. These biochemical imbalances appear to be highly ________________ and can be treated by drugs such as ________________ carbonate. (474)

SCHIZOPHRENIA

1 **half** **perception** **thinking**

15. Schizophrenia affects approximately ________________ percent of the American population and accounts for ________________ the patients confined to mental institutions. The hallmarks of schizophrenia are serious alterations of activity, ________________, emotion, and ________________. (474)

behavior **catatonic** **agitation/paranoid** **unrealistic**

16. The subtypes of schizophrenia are as follows: (1) disorganized schizophrenics show bizarre ________________; (2) ________________ schizophrenics may show either extreme immobility or ________________; (3) ________________ schizophrenics are plagued by ________________ fears and suspicions; and (4) undifferentiated schizophrenics—schizophrenics who cannot be fit into the other classifications. (475)

persecution **grandeur**

17. Three types of delusions include delusions of ________________, ideas of reference, and delusions of ________________. (475)

associations

18. Schizophrenic thought may contain made-up words and loose ________________, such as clang associations. (476)

relevant/irrelevant

19. Schizophrenics find it especially difficult to differentiate between ________________ and ________________ information and are easily

distracted

________, which may be at the heart of schizophrenic thought disorders. (476)

stressful/reactive
slowly
disturbing/less

20. Schizophrenia which strikes suddenly in reaction to a ________ event is called ________ schizophrenia, while process schizophrenia develops very ________, appears less ________, and is ________ likely to be overcome. (476)

50
dopamine
emotional

21. If one identical twin has schizophrenia, there is about a ________ percent chance the other twin will experience the disorder. Schizophrenia is associated with an overproduction of the transmitter substance ________, which transmits messages to portions of the limbic system that regulate ________ responses. (477)

says
means

22. Another theory holds that schizophrenia develops from double-bind communications in one's family, in which a person ________ one thing, but ________ another. (477)

exclusive

23. The various explanations of schizophrenia are not mutually ________. (478)

more
alienated

24. Laing (1967) believes some schizophrenics are ________ sane than normal people, who are ________ from themselves. (479)

THE DISORDERS OF CHILDHOOD

rules/boys
aggression/Anxiety
relations

25. Conduct disorders are marked by repeated violations of social ________, occur mostly among ________, and often involve ________. ________ disorders are marked by excessive worrying. Child onset pervasive developmental disorders involve profound disturbance in ________ with others and bizarre behavior. (479)

attention
3/5
ten
will not
is not
norepinephrine/dopamine
Stimulants
conflicting

26. Hyperactivity is now called ________ deficit disorder, and affects ________ to ________ percent of all children, with boys outnumbering girls ________ to one. A hyperactive 4-month-old baby ________ stop moving when it sees someone's face. The cause of hyperactivity ________ known, but, as in depression, often involves the depletion of the transmitters ________ and ________. ________ such as Ritalin increase the levels of the neurotransmitters. Studies on the effectiveness of Ritalin have produced ________ results. (480)

10,000
male
first
isolation/sameness
language
left
modification
intelligence/speaking
2

27. Infantile autism affects fewer than 1 out of every ________ children, and are more likely to be ________ and ________-borns. The predominant signs are self-imposed ________, insistence on ________ in the environment, and gross ________ difficulties. Autism is probably a disorder in the brain's ________ hemisphere. Treatment centers on behavior ________ procedures. The long-term outlook for the autistic child is most closely linked with ________ and ________ ability; only ________ percent recover to be normal. (480)

PSYCHOLOGICAL ISSUE: *SUICIDE*

third
homicides
increasing
less
more
age
married
less
faster

28. Suicide ranks tenth among causes of death for adults and is ________ as a cause of death among college students, after accidents and ________. Suicide rates have been ________, especially for adolescents. Males are ________ likely to attempt suicide and are ________ likely to succeed. Suicide rates for men increase with ________; the rate goes down for women after 54. The suicide rate is lowest for persons who are ________. Blacks are significantly ________ likely to commit suicide, but the suicide rate for blacks is rising ________ than that of whites. (487)

achievements/expectations

29. Seiden (1966) concludes college students commit suicide because their ________ don't measure up to their ________. (488)

dissipates

30. According to Seligman (1975) the roots of suicide are in depression, which ________ in time. (489)

Self-Quiz

1. The suicide rate is lowest for people who are:
- **a.** single.
- **b.** married
- **c.** divorced.
- **d.** widowed.

2. Which statement is false?
- **a.** Anxiety is vaguer than fear.
- **b.** Fear and anxiety have different physiological manifestations.
- **c.** The obsessive-compulsive person is attempting to master a threat.
- **d.** Extreme neatness may be a reaction formation.

3. Psychotics are characterized by all but which one of the following?
- **a.** They have largely lost contact with reality.
- **b.** They may experience hallucinations and delusions.
- **c.** They may have lost control over their emotions.
- **d.** They are a minority of people confined to mental hospitals.

4. Which statement is not true of depression?
- **a.** Depression is probably the most susceptible of all psychological disorders to effective treatment.
- **b.** Students who confront problems are less depressed.
- **c.** Depression is probably caused by too much serotonin, norepinephrine, or dopamine.
- **d.** Depression can be treated with lithium carbonate.

5. Phobias are particularly common in:
- **a.** childhood.

b. adolescence.
c. adulthood.
d. old age.

6. A person who attempts to master a threat by repeatedly engaging in behavior connected with the threat is:
a. wise.
b. obsessive-compulsive.
c. psychotic.
d. manic-depressive.

7. Dissociative disorders are characterized by all but which one of the following?
a. They include amnesia, fugue states, and multiple personality.
b. In amnesia, a person retains his or her talents and knowledge.
c. In fugue states, a person starts a new life in a different location.
d. They are a fairly common type of disorder.

8. Which one of the following statements is not true?
a. Schizophrenia affects approximately 1 percent of the U.S. population.
b. The most common psychological problem is depression.
c. There may be a hereditary basis for obsessive-compulsive disorders.
d. There may be a hereditary basis for phobias.

9. Which statement is not true of schizophrenia?
a. Disorganized schizophrenics exhibit bizarre behavior.
b. Undifferentiated schizophrenics quickly recover.
c. Catatonic schizophrenics may either remain immobilized or show agitation.
d. Paranoid schizophrenics appear normal, but have overblown fears and suspicions.

10. Which one of the following statements is not true of schizophrenia?
a. Process schizophrenia strikes suddenly.
b. The process schizophrenic seems less disturbed than the reactive schizophrenic.
c. The reactive schizophrenic is more likely to recover.
d. There is probably no single cause for either type of schizophrenia.

Answers: 1.b 2.b 3.d 4.c 5.a 6.b 7.d 8.c 9.b 10.a

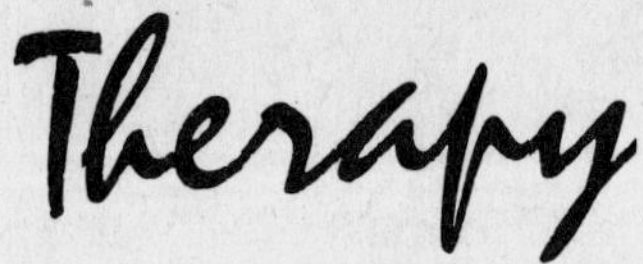

Therapy

1. Distinguish between therapy and counseling. List the goals shared by all therapies. (491)

INSIGHT THERAPIES

2. Define insight therapy. Describe the case of Anna O. Show how it illustrates the basis of psychoanalysis. (492)

3. Describe each of the following and its role in psychoanalysis: (493)

   Catharsis—

   Free association—

   Resistance—

   Interpretation—

Transference—

4. What was Freud's view of the therapist's role? Compare traditional psychoanalysis with recent trends. Who would benefit least and most from psychoanalysis? (493)

5. *BOX 1:* Summarize the aims and goals of Gestalt therapy. List Perls's three rules for living. (496)

6. *BOX 1:* What is the role of nonverbal clues and physical communication in Gestalt therapy. Define psychodrama. What is the Gestalt philosophy? Why has Gestalt therapy been criticized? (496)

7. What is the aim of client-centered therapy? Describe unconditional positive regard. (495)

8. What is the client-centered therapist's main task? What are the most important factors in successful therapy? What does research on these factors reveal? (499)

BEHAVIOR THERAPIES

9. Describe: (497)

Behavior therapies—

Desensitization therapy—

Counterconditioning—

Systematic desensitization—

Anxiety hierarchy—

10. Describe the Freeling and Shemberg study. (498)

11. Define operant therapy. Cite two examples. List two ways to maintain change after reinforcement ceases. (499)

12. Define modeling and role playing, giving examples. Summarize the Christensen and Arkowitz study. How does the concept of *cognitive restructuring* reflect current thinking? (501)

13. *BOX 2:* What is the basis of *RET,* and how does it differ from other therapies? Describe the RET therapist's job. What is the major criticism of RET? (502)

SOMATIC THERAPIES

14. Define somatic therapy, psychopharmacology, and antianxiety drugs. Describe the recent history of the use of antianxiety drugs. (503)

15. Define antidepressant drugs and tricyclics. How do they work? Describe lithium carbonate and its effects. (504)

16. Define antipsychotic drugs. Describe phenothiazines and their effects. What is the controversy about phenothiazines? Define tardive dyskinesia. (505)

17. *BOX 3:* Describe the movement for deinstitutionalization and the two factors that brought it about. How well has the goal of reducing patient population been met? (507)

18. *BOX 3:* What are the problems with deinstitutionalization? What is being done to solve the problem of revolving-door admissions? (507)

19. How is electroshock therapy administered? How widely used is it? For what disorders is it used? What are the side effects? (506)

20. Define psychosurgery. What were the results of prefrontal lobotomies? Describe the current frequency and use of psychosurgery. (508)

DOES THERAPY WORK?

21. Compare Eysenck's conclusion with the current conclusion about psychotherapy. Summarize the method, results, and conclusions of Sloane's study. (509)

22. List Luborsky's conclusions about what makes psychotherapy work. Summarize the evidence for these conclusions. (509)

23. Define eclectic. What does Frank believe about the effectiveness of different therapies? What is the role of expectations in therapy? (510)

24. *BOX 4:* Describe: (510)

Community mental health centers—

Crisis intervention—

Self-help groups—

Peer (paraprofessional) counseling—

THERAPY AND RESPONSIBILITY

25. List the responsibilities of the therapist and the client in therapy. (512)

PSYCHOLOGICAL ISSUE: *THE THERAPY MARKETPLACE*

26. Define the following terms, distinguishing them from each other: (516)

Primal therapy—

Scream therapy—

Rebirthing—

Encounter groups—

est–

Transpersonal therapies—

27. Describe the Stanford University study. What is the criticism of alternative therapies? (518)

28. Describe self-help books and "therapists on the airwaves." What conclusions do the authors draw about these developments? (519)

Self-Quiz

1. The psychoanalytic notion that the clients will act toward the therapist as they act toward significant other persons in their lives is known as:
   a. resistance.
   b. interpretation.
   c. working through.
   d. transference. (Study Question 3)

2. The Rogerian notion that the therapist respects the client no matter what he or she does or says is called:
   a. unconditional positive regard.
   b. transference.
   c. sympathetic interplay.
   d. conditional positive empathy. (Study Question 7)

3. According to behavior therapists, fear of flying could best be unlearned through:
   a. psychoanalysis.
   b. desensitization.
   c. somatic therapy.
   d. token economy. (Study Question 9)

4. Operant therapy:
   a. looks for the deep, underlying causes of psychological problems.
   b. tries to draw out repressed emotions and thoughts.
   c. uses positive reinforcement and concentrates on behavior.
   d. primarily gives the client unconditional positive regard. (Study Question 11)

5. Benzodiazepines such as Valium and Librium are:
   a. antidepressant drugs.
   b. antischizophrenic drugs.
   c. antianxiety drugs.
   d. antipsychotic drugs. (Study Question 14)

6. Deinstitutionalization:
   a. is inconsistent with the community mental health movement.
   b. has progressed much slower than expected.
   c. began in the 1970s.
   d. was facilitated by the introduction of antipsychotic drugs. (Study Question 17)

7. Electroshock is used primarily for:
   a. neurosis.
   b. dissociative reaction.
   c. amnesia.
   d. none of the above. (Study Question 19)

8. Which one of the following statements is not true of the effectiveness of therapy?
   a. Eysenck pointed out that many patients improved simply with the passage of time.
   b. The Sloane study found subjects in behavior therapy, psychoanalytic therapy, and no therapy all improved over a four month period.
   c. Subjects in the two treatment groups improved more than the waiting list clients in the Sloane study.
   d. Behavior therapy was more effective than psychoanalytic therapy in the Sloane study. (Study Question 21)

9. To call a therapist *eclectic* is to say that he or she is:
   a. rigid in therapeutic technique.
   b. flexible in therapeutic technique.
   c. a specialist in the treatment of specific disorders.
   d. a paraprofessional. (Study Question 23)

10. The therapy during which clients experience the "creeping crud" is:
   a. encounter group therapy.
   b. primal therapy.
   c. rebirthing.
   d. transpersonal therapy. (Study Question 26)

Answers to Self-Quiz: 1.d 2.a 3.b 4.c 5.c 6.d 7.d 8.d 9.b 10.c

Programmed Review Unit

6 1. It is estimated that some ________ million Americans receive
therapy each year. (490)
decisions 2. Counseling focuses on specific ________ or adjustments that a
person needs to make, whereas therapy is concerned with more
generalized/deeper-rooted ________ or ________ psychological
problems. (491)
3. All therapeutic approaches share the goals of: (1) giving the client relief
anxiety from ________, symptoms, and conflict; (2) establishing
maturity personal ________, feelings of adequacy, and
integrity ________ of the different parts of the self; (3) improving
interpersonal ________ relationships; and (4) adjusting satisfactorily to the
culture/society ________ and ________. (491)

INSIGHT THERAPIES

discussion 4. The basic idea of insight therapies is that open ________ of
problems can bring insight into its causes and possible
solutions ________; these therapies particularly emphasize expression
feelings of inner ________. (492)
5. Psychoanalysis and client-centered therapy differ greatly in their
theoretical ________ basis and in their approach to the
client-therapist ________ relationship. (492)

unconscious
emotions
catharsis
free association
interpretation
transference
mirror
eclectic
schizophrenic
anxiety/depressions

6. The goal of psychoanalysis is to open the doors to the ________ and release pent-up ________. The ultimate emotional release, called ________, is reached through such techniques as ________, in which clients are asked to say whatever comes into their minds. In the process of ________ the analyst points out resistances and offers some reasons for them. If the patient shifts her or his emotions from past relationships to focus them on the therapist, ________ has occurred. Freud felt the therapist should be a ________ of what the patient reveals. Contemporary psychoanalytic therapists tend to be ________, borrowing techniques from other therapies when appropriate. Psychoanalytic therapy is not effective with ________ or other psychotic patients, and Freud felt it is most useful for people with ________ disorders or relatively mild ________. (492)

here and now
whole
entire
feeling
how
psychodrama
responsible

7. Gestalt therapy emphasizes awareness of the ________. *Gestalt* means "arrangement of the parts in a ________." The aim of Gestalt therapy is to put people in touch with their ________ self and with their surroundings. Gestalt therapy stresses ________ rather than thinking. Perls (1969) felt it was more important to ask ________ than to ask why questions. Gestalt therapy uses ________, in which one acts out scenes in order to bring out their emotional significance. Gestalt therapy takes the view that people are ________ for their own lives and can make their own choices. (496)

unconditional positive
interpret
warmth/empathy
supported

8. Client-centered therapists help individuals express and experience their true feelings by providing ________ regard. Unlike the psychoanalyst, the client-centered therapist does not try to ________; that job is left to the client. According to Rogers, ________ and ________ from the therapist are the most important factors in the success of therapy; this is ________ by studies on the effectiveness of various therapies. (495)

BEHAVIOR THERAPIES

experimental
learning
emotions or thoughts
inappropriate
skills

9. The behavior therapies are based on the principles of ________ psychology, especially of ________ theory, do not look for deep underlying causes for psychological problems, and do not see therapy as a process of drawing out buried ________. Behavior therapy seeks to help the client "unlearn" ________ or unsatisfactory behaviors and to replace them with appropriate ones, and to help the client acquire the ________ needed to cope effectively. (497)

feared
stimulus
responses
imagine
relax
reduce

10. Desensitization therapy links ________ objects or situations with new responses that replace the fear. Counterconditioning occurs when the fearful ________ is repeatedly paired with an object that produces positive, nonfearful ________. In systematic desensitization, Wolpe (1958) had subjects ________ a hierarchy of increasingly anxiety-provoking events, while simultaneously learning to ________. Freeling and Shemberg (1970) found that students could ________ test anxiety using desensitization techniques. (497)

classical positive motivate desired existing complex 60	**11.** Whereas desensitization was suggested by the principles of ________ conditioning, operant therapy relies heavily on operant conditioning principles, particularly ________ reinforcement. Bandura (1967) feels the reward must be something that will ________ the client, must be contingent on performance of the ________ behavior, and must be accompanied by a method for gradually molding ________ behaviors into more ________ behaviors not yet in the person's repertoire. Using a teacher's attention as a reinforcer, a boy in a nursery school who spent about 80 percent of his time playing alone was shaped into spending ________ percent of his time with others, which eventually became a self-reinforcing behavior. (499)
modeling fears desired/protective feedback assertiveness restructuring	**12.** One of the best ways to acquire a new response or skill is to watch another person demonstrate it—this is called ________, and is useful in overcoming ________ of snakes, dogs, dentists, and so forth. This is often augmented by role playing, in which a person practices a ________ behavior in a ________ setting, and gets ________ on his performance. Both modeling and role playing are often used in programs of ________ training. Cognitive ________ involves modification of one's thoughts. (501)

SOMATIC THERAPIES

drugs physiological tranquilizers depression addiction sedative norepinephrine bipolar major schizophrenia cure dopamine/limbic cerebral	**13.** Somatic therapy is the use of ________, electric shocks, or other ________ means to treat the symptoms of a psychological disorder. Antianxiety drugs (also known as minor ________) include barbiturates—strong sedatives that cause drowsiness and sometimes ________ and ________, as well as have the potential for lethal overdose. Benzodiazepines do not have a ________ effect. Antidepressant drugs include the tricyclics, which increase the level of the neurotransmitter ________. Lithium carbonate is extremely successful in moderating the highs of ________ disorders. Antipsychotic drugs (or ________ tranquilizers) include phenothiazines, which relieve the agitation, delusions, and thought disorders that beset ________; they do not ________ the underlying disorder. Researchers' best guess about the primary cause of schizophrenia is an excess of the transmitter ________ in the ________ system and the ________ cortex. (503)
irrational/events expectations/illogical emotions rational directive	**14.** Rational-emotive therapy assumes that emotional difficulties are caused by ________ thinking, rather than ________ themselves. The disturbed person's belief system may contain unrealistic ________ or ________ reasoning. Ellis (in Gross, 1978) feels that letting out one's ________ is rarely curative, and instead suggests cognitive restructuring—developing more ________ beliefs. Unlike psychoanalytic and client-centered therapies, RET is highly ________. (502)
long-term/5	**15.** The majority of hospitalized mental patients suffer from ________ disorders. Only about ________ percent

of all patients hospitalized for longer than two years were eventually discharged. However, recently there is a shift toward

deinstitutionalization/65 ________________. This has led to a ________________ percent decrease in the mental patient population of state hospitals between 1955 and 1975. The average number of days spent in the hospital decreased by

two-thirds/half more than ________________. However, about ________________ of the discharged patients are readmitted within a year. A well-run San

75 Jose, California, program caused ________________ percent of the patients to feel they had benefitted from community living. (507)

16. Electroshock treatments is successful in alleviating the symptoms of

depression/overused severe ________________; however, it is ________________. (506)

Psychosurgery 17. ________________ refers to the surgical destruction or disconnection of

brain portions of the ________________ in an attempt to regulate disordered

were not behavior. The results of prefrontal lobotomies ________________

irreversible encouraging. The effects of psychosurgery are ________________. (508)

DOES THERAPY WORK?

18. Eysenck (1952) claimed that no more patients improved with

psychoanalytic psychotherapy (mainly ________________) than would have improved

time with the passage of ________________. But recent studies indicate that

positive on the average psychotherapy tends to have modest ________________ effects. After long months of receiving either short-term psychoanalytic therapy, behavior therapy, or no therapy, on the average clients in all

improved these groups ________________. Clients in the two treatment groups

more improved ________________ than the waiting-list clients. (509)

19. The best predictions of whether a particular client will improve are the

client's ________________ characteristics: those who are relatively healthy,

intelligent/motivated ________________, and highly ________________ are most likely to make effective use of therapy. Of least importance are the characteristics

therapy of the particular type of ________________. Strupp and Hadley (1979)

understanding found that professors who formed ________________ relationships

psychotherapists helped students just as much as highly experienced ________________. Systematic desensitization is especially useful in treating

phobias ________________. The key features of the different types of successful

close therapies are a ________________ relationship between therapist and client, the special setting, and the powerful influence of

expectations ________________. (510)

20. The idea that people with problems are often best helped in their own

community/650 ________________ has led to the establishment of ________________ federally funded community mental health centers. Services include

crisis/self-help ________________ intervention with hotlines and ________________

paraprofessionals groups. Services often employ ________________, community residents trained by professionals to provide therapy or support. (510)

THERAPY AND RESPONSIBILITY

21. Frank (1973) feels that "Psychotherapy is the only form of treatment

create which, at least to some extent, appears to ________________ the illness

	it treats." The prospective client needs to assume responsibility for deciding what sort of help she or he needs, choosing a therapist or
actively	treatment facility, participating ________________ in her or his own
discontinue	treatment, and to ________________ therapy if she or he feels it is not helping. (510)

PSYCHOLOGICAL ISSUE: ***THE THERAPY MARKETPLACE***

130	**22.** There are now at least ________________ different forms of therapy available, which have in common the stated goals of reducing
problems/happiness	psychological ________________ and increasing ________________ and self-fulfillment. Janov's primal therapy centers on the idea of
pain	________________. The aim of encounter groups is to bring people
openness	together to increase trust, ________________, and sensitivity. The
It	"________________" of *est* remains undefined. One of the problems with evaluating therapeutic claims is that it is difficult to define
success	________________. Lieberman, Yalom, and Miles (1973) found
one-third	________________ of the college students showed positive effects of
one-third	encounter groups, ________________ showed negative effects, and
no	one-third showed ________________ effects; generally encounter
control	subjects showed no more change than ________________ subjects.
books	Recently, there has been a proliferation of self-help ________________, as well as programs on the airwaves. However, the APA Ethical Standards do not support giving psychological services in the
media	________________. Frunk (1972) attributes the sudden flow of
upheaval	alternative therapies to the current ________________ in society. (518)

Self-Quiz

1. Electroshock treatments have been particularly helpful in treating:
a. nervous tics.
b. obsessions.
c. depression.
d. phobias.

2. Which statement is not true of the Sloane study on the effectiveness of therapy?
a. People who received no therapy improved.
b. Short-term psychoanalytic therapy was more effective than no therapy.
c. Behavior therapy was more effective than no therapy.
d. Behavior therapy was more effective than psychoanalytic therapy.

3. Behavior therapy may be especially useful for treating:
a. nervous tics.
b. obsessions.
c. depression.
d. phobias.

4. Which statement is not true of alternative psychotherapies?
a. *est* has clearly defined what "getting It" means.
b. Encounter groups encourage openness.

c. Janov focuses on childhood pain.
d. Alternative therapies have in common the goal of increasing personal happiness.

5. The key features of successful therapies include all but which one of the following?
   a. Close relationship between therapist and client.
   b. Use of medication.
   c. Special setting.
   d. The influence of expectations.

6. Rational-emotive therapy is characterized by all but which one of the following?
   a. Emotional difficulties are assumed to be the result of irrational thinking.
   b. RET is nondirective.
   c. Ellis feels that letting out one's emotions is rarely curative.
   d. Ellis recommends developing more rational beliefs.

7. What proportion of the students in the Lieberman, Yalom, and Miles study showed negative effects of being in encounter groups?
   a. 1 percent.
   b. 10 percent.
   c. 25 percent.
   d. 33 percent.

8. Which statement is not true?
   a. Client-centered therapists give unconditional positive regard to a client.
   b. Psychoanalysts attempt to be neutral.
   c. Client-centered therapists interpret a client's comments.
   d. Psychoanalysts interpret a client's comments.

9. The general goals of therapy include all but which one of the following?
   a. Relief from anxiety.
   b. Better integration of the parts of the self.
   c. Better attainment of personal goals.
   d. Improvement of interpersonal relations.

10. Which statement is not true?
    a. Transference involves shifting the client's feeling about others onto the therapist.
    b. Prefrontal lobotomies have produced encouraging results.
    c. Electroshock treatments cause memory loss.
    d. One ethical issue in psychotherapy is over the extent to which therapy may create the problem it seeks to cure.

Answers: 1.c 2.d 3.d 4.a 5.b 6.b 7.d 8.c 9.c 10.b

Chapter 17

Female and Male

PSYCHOLOGICAL DIFFERENCES BETWEEN MEN AND WOMEN

1. How are physical and psychological differences between women and men related to the roles of women and men? (523)

2. Define stereotype. Describe Broverman's study. How are stereotypes misleading? Describe the Deaux and Emswiler study. (524)

3. *BOX 1:* What is psychology's sex bias? What is the evidence for it? How might it perpetuate stereotypes? (526)

4. Identify Maccoby and Jacklin. List sex differences that they discovered to be myths and those that have been reliably established. (525)

5. Considering the evidence, what is the safe conclusion regarding psychological sex differences? (527)

6. Describe two reasons for the perpetuation of stereotypic sex differences. (527)

EXPLAINING THE DIFFERENCES: BIOLOGY AND CULTURE

7. What is the cross-cultural evidence on sex differences in aggression? How does this evidence show whether the differences are biological? (529)

8. What is the evidence from animals with respect to biological differences in aggression? (529)

9. Explain the prenatal development of sexual differentiation. How is this related to temperament and behavior. What evidence is presented by Young et al? (529)

10. Define prenatal androgenization. Describe the Ehrhardt and Baker study and its conclusions. (529)

11. Define predispositions. How does human behavior reflect them? Summarize the evidence for the cultural shaping of aggression. What is the overall conclusion concerning biology and culture? (531)

12. Distinguish between sex roles and stereotypes. How are sex roles learned at home and in school? (532)

13. How is sex-role learning an active process? Describe the role of television in sex-role learning. (534)

HUMAN SEXUALITY

14. Contrast the sexual attitudes of Mangaia with those of Inis Beag. What is the Victorian-era effect on our culture? Define double standard. (539)

15. How did Freud promote the double standard? Summarize the impact of Kinsey's study. List two ways to measure the sexual revolution. (540)

16. *BOX 3:* How has sexual behavior on campus changed? What evidence is there that the double standard still prevails? What pressures result from permissive sexual attitudes? (542)

17. Describe the four stages of sexual arousal. What was the most important finding of Masters and Johnson? How do men and women differ with respect to the refractory period? (535)

18. Summarize the following evidence on the importance of cognitive factors in sexual arousal: the effects of fantasy, Heiman's study, Geer and Fuhr's study, and the causes of sexual dysfunction. (538)

19. List two forces behind the sexual revolution. Summarize the positive and negative effects of the sexual revolution. (542)

PSYCHOLOGICAL ISSUE: *CHANGING SEX ROLES*

20. Describe: (548)

    Sexism—

    Goldberg's study—

    The Feminine Mystique—

    Goals of the women's movement—

21. What are the most significant gains made by women and what problems remain? List the concerns of men's liberation. (551)

22. What did Henley conclude in studying the politics of touch? Define psychological androgyny. What were Bem's findings? (553)

Self-Quiz

1. Deaux and Emswiler found that good performance on a task involving the identification of mechanical objects was considered to be due to outstanding skill when:
   a. the task was said to be oriented toward females.
   b. the task was said to be oriented toward males.
   c. the performer was said to be a male.
   d. the performer was said to be a female. (Study Question 2)

2. Studies of psychological sex differences reveal that there is good evidence that:
   a. boys are more independent.
   b. girls are more nurturant.

c. boys are more aggressive.
d. none of the above. (Study Question 4)

3. Stereotypical differences between the sexes are perpetuated because:
a. they are true more often than not.
b. our perception of people and their behavior is selective, and society provides traditionally different opportunities for men and women.
c. psychologists are unable to change them, and men and women behave predictably.
d. none of the above. (Study Question 6)

4. The data concerning male predisposition toward aggressive behavior indicates that ________________ levels in the individual's system may promote such behavior.
a. testosterone
b. estrogen
c. ACTH
d. progesterone (Study Question 9)

5. Expectations about what men and women ought to be are called:
a. postures.
b. role expectations.
c. stereotypes.
d. sex roles. (Study Question 12)

6. The effect of the Victorian era on our culture has been to:
a. promote the sexual revolution.
b. counter the influence of the double standard.
c. strongly influence our current sexual attitudes.
d. all of the above. (Study Question 14)

7. Freud's view of sex:
a. was that it was only a secondary motivational force.
b. promoted the double standard.
c. helped establish that sexual desire was abnormal.
d. divorced sex from the desire to have children. (Study Question 15)

8. Sexual behavior on campus in recent years:
a. has liberated men but put strong pressures on women.
b. has put strong pressures on both men and women.
c. has liberated women but put strong pressures on men.
d. has been fully liberating for both men and women. (Study Question 16)

9. According to the text, two major forces behind the emphasis on sexual enjoyment in the 1970s are:
a. Masters and Johnson's research and Kinsey's research.
b. Freud and humanistic psychology.
c. Humanistic psychology and Masters and Johnson's research.
d. Kinsey's research and Freud. (Study Question 19)

10. An experiment by Bem found that which type of student could behave effectively and appropriately in a greater variety of situations?
 a. A highly masculine student.
 b. A highly feminine student.
 c. An androgynous student.
 d. A female student. (Study Question 22)

Answers to Self-Quiz: 1.c 2.c 3.b 4.a 5.d 6.c 7.b 8.b 9.c 10.c

Programmed Review Unit

PSYCHOLOGICAL DIFFERENCES BETWEEN MEN AND WOMEN

Males
shorter
stereotypes
aggressive/dominant
competitive/confident
tactful
emotional/quiet
overgeneralize/bias
skillful
assume

1. ________ are more likely to be colorblind and live ________ lives. In Broverman's (1972) survey on sexual ________, men were described as being more ________, independent, active, ________, ________, and self-________ than women, who were described as being more ________, gentle, sensitive, ________, expressive, neat, and ________. These stereotypes are misleading, because they encourage us to ________, and can lead to a ________ in the way we evaluate people's work. Subjects in Deaux and Enswiler's (1974) study thought the same work was more ________ when done by a man. The stereotype that men are more mechanical led subjects to ________ the man's performance reflected greater ability. (523)

similar
influenced
unsure

2. Maccoby and Jacklin (1974) concluded that males and females are basically ________. Eagly (1978) found that women are not more easily ________ than men, and that both sexes are influenced to the extent they feel ________ in a particular sphere. (525)

more
stereotypes

3. Males are used as subjects ________ often than females, which means that research has perpetuated ________. (526)

aggressive/verbal
spatial/mathematical
feelings

4. There is evidence that, on the average, males are more ________, have less ________ ability and greater ________ and ________ ability than females. There is also evidence that females are more concerned about other people's ________. (526)

unexpected
Myths
opportunities

5. When someone behaves in an ________ way, the behavior may go unnoticed or may be passed off as a fluke. ________ about sexual differences are also perpetuated by the different ________ that our society provides for men and women. (527)

EXPLAINING THE DIFFERENCES: BIOLOGY AND CULTURE

6. The tendency for males to be more aggressive is probably determined by

biology/culture	an interaction between __________ and __________,
hormones	specifically between male __________ and social influences.
rare	There is evidence that the __________ occurrences of prenatal
	androgenization (where a genetic female has added male hormones) may
behavior	have an effect on a woman's __________. Tomboyish behavior is
normal	__________ for girls. (530)
predisposition	**7.** A __________ is a readiness to behave or develop in a particular
	way. But whether someone will behave aggresively, for example,
situation	depends greatly on the particular __________. Ember (1973)
	found that boys among the Luo who were assigned to do female work
less	tended to be __________ aggressive and dominant and more
dependent	__________ than other boys. Under some conditions, women are
aggressive/biological	just as __________ as men. It seems that the __________
	boundaries are extremely broad, and that any psychological differences
	between men and women are shaped to a much greater extent by
culture	__________. (531)
	8. Whereas stereotypes are widely held assumptions of what men and
like	women are __________, sex roles are widely held notions about
ought to be	the way men and women __________. By the time children are
work	in kindergarten they usually know what sorts of __________ are
	for men and what sorts are for women. Virtually all children learn their
3	sex by age __________. A great deal of sex-role learning takes place
media/television	through the __________, especially __________. (532)

HUMAN SEXUALITY

	9. Recent research has shown that the physiology of sex in men and women
similar	is much more __________ than had been suspected. (535)
did not	**10.** Freud's views __________ influence the double standard. Freud
heterosexual intercourse	also thought that __________ was the only psychologically
	mature form of sex. Kinsey (1948, 1953) found that in contrast to 1900,
premarital	people in 1950 were more inclined to engage in __________
guilty	intercourse. People now are less likely to feel __________ about
	engaging in sex. (540)
	11. Katz and Cronin (1980) estimate that the average age of first intercourse
17	is now __________. There has been a greater increase in
women	premarital intercourse for __________; however
males	__________ are still more often the initiator of sex. (542)
	12. Masters and Johnson (1966) describe the sexual response for men and
	women as going through the same four stages, which are (in order): 1) the
excitement/plateau	__________ phase; 2) the __________ phase; 3) the
orgasmic/resolution	__________ phase; and 4) the __________ phase.
refractory	Women may skip the __________ period after orgasm, during
	which further excitement to orgasm is impossible. For humans, sex is as
cognitive	much __________ and psychological as it is genital. Heiman
	(1975) found that sexual stimuli occurs largely above the
neck/stimuli	__________ and in the presence of the same __________
	for men and women. Geer and Fuhr (1976) found that people have to
pay attention	__________ to get sexually aroused. Sexual dysfunction includes
intercourse/enjoy	inability to perform __________, to __________ sex, to

orgasm/ejaculation	reach ________, or, in males, to delay ________.
physical	Very few sexual dysfunctions are caused by ________
worrying	problems; a major contributor to sexual dysfunction is
	________. (535)
	13. Hunt (1974) found that the average duration for sexual intercourse for
ten	married couples has increased to ________ minutes. People
foreplay	are also showing more variations in sexual ________ and
positions	________. (542)
adolescent	**14.** There has been an increase in unwanted ________
20	pregnancies; no more than ________ percent of the sexually
	active 15- to 19-year-olds use contraceptives regularly. One in
six	________ of sexually active college women reported having
abortion	undergone an ________ at some time. (543)
	15. There is a danger that the sexual revolution can give people
new	________ anxieties and insecurities. (544)

PSYCHOLOGICAL ISSUE: *CHANGING SEX ROLES*

	16. Sexism is the view that the sexes not only are different but are inherently
unequal	________. A survey of jokes in *Reader's Digest* in the 1940s
six	through 1960s found ________ times as many antifemale jokes
	as antimale ones. Goldberg (1968) found that the same article was given
significantly	________ lower ratings when it was supposedly written by a
woman	________. The Bems (1970) suggest that male superiority has
	become a set of assumptions that we do not specifically
acknowledge	________, even to ourselves. The major goals of the women's
pay	movement have included equal ________ for equal
work/job	________, an end to ________ discrimination by
child-care	sex, adequate ________ programs, an equal sharing of
family	________ responsibilities, and the right to
abortion	________. More women than men entered college for the first
1978	time in U.S. history in ________. The number of women law
tripled	students ________ between 1972 and 1978. In 1980, about
50	________ percent of all women worked outside the home.
57	Women still only make ________ cents for every dollar men
	make. When significant numbers of men enter a formerly "female"
rise	occupation, salaries are likely to ________. By the end of the
majority	1970s a ________ of Americans favored greater equality for the
	sexes. (549)
	17. The men's liberation movement is especially concerned with helping men
competitive	to relate to one another in a less ________ way. There is
no	________ evidence that men have less capacity to be nurturant
	or form bonds with infants. (551)
more	**18.** Men talk ________ than women and interrupt women
more	________ than vice versa. According to Henley (1977), the
higher/touching	________-status person initiates ________ the
lower	________-status person. There is evidence that
females	________ are touched more, which appears to be the trend
1	even before they are age ________. (552)
healthiest	**19.** The ________ people are not those who are highly

	"masculine" males or highly "feminine" females. Bem (1972, 1975) calls the ability to combine "masculine" and "feminine" traits psychological
androgyny	________________. Androgynous students behaved more
effectively	________________ in a variety of situations than students who were highly masculine or highly feminine. (553)

Self-Quiz

1. Which statement is not true?
   a. Stereotypes encourage us to overgeneralize.
   b. Overgeneralization can lead to bias.
   c. The same work was thought by observers to be equally skillful regardless of which sexed person did the work.
   d. Males and females have similar patterns of sexual response.

2. There is evidence for which of the following?
   a. Boys are more independent.
   b. Boys are more aggressive.
   c. Boys are more ambitious.
   d. All of the above.

3. There is evidence for which of the following?
   a. Boys are more achievement-oriented.
   b. Girls are more nurturant.
   c. Girls are more sociable.
   d. None of the above.

4. There is evidence for all but which one of the following?
   a. Girls are more influenced.
   b. Girls have less spatial ability.
   c. Boys have more mathematical ability.
   d. Girls have more verbal ability.

5. Which one of the following statements is not true?
   a. Prenatal androgenization occurs when a female had extra male hormones.
   b. Prenatal androgenization is rare.
   c. Prenatal androgenization may have an effect on a woman's behavior.
   d. Tomboyish behavior is probably caused by prenatal androgenization.

6. Which statement is not true of the women's liberation movement?
   a. Sexism is the view that the sexes are inherently unequal.
   b. It seeks to become liberated from nonconscious ideology.
   c. Its goals include equal pay for equal work.
   d. It does not seek increased access to abortion.

7. Which one of the following statements is not true?
   a. The men's liberation movement seeks to help men relate to one another in a less competitive way.

b. The healthiest people are very masculine or very feminine.
c. Androgynous people are more able to be flexible.
d. Males have been used as subjects in social psychology studies more often than females.

8. Which statement is not true?
   a. The goals of the women's liberation movement include putting down men.
   b. Females are more concerned than males about other people's feelings, on the average.
   c. The average full-time female worker earns 57 percent of what the average full-time male worker earns.
   d. Males have the same capacity for nurturance as females.

9. Children learn what sorts of work are for men and what sorts are for women by what age?
   a. 3.
   b. Nursery school.
   c. Kindergarten.
   d. Third grade.

10. Which one of the following statements is not true?
    a. Psychological differences between males and females are shaped more by biology than by culture.
    b. There has been an increase in unwanted adolescent pregnancies.
    c. The same article was rated lower when thought to be written by a woman.
    d. Considerable sex-role learning takes place through television.

Answers: 1.c 2.b 3.d 4.a 5.d 6.d 7.b 8.a 9.c 10.a

Chapter 18

Attitudes and Influence

COMPONENTS OF ATTITUDES: THOUGHTS AND FEELINGS

1. Define and distinguish among the following: (555)

Attitude—

Cognitive component—

Affective component—

MEASURING ATTITUDES

2. Describe open-ended and fixed-response techniques. Why do fixed-response measures often use more than one question? (556)

3. What has been the fate of physiological measures of attitudes? Describe Hess's technique. (556)

4. List the problems in attitude measurement. Describe the Shomer and Centers study and its conclusions. (557)

WHERE DO ATTITUDES COME FROM?

5. How do commercials illustrate the emotional foundations of attitudes? Explain how classical conditioning applies in this instance. (557)

6. Describe the cognitive foundation of attitudes in terms of the following: (559)

   Horizontal structure—

   Vertical structure—

   Consistency—

7. How do children develop attitudes? Describe the method and results of Newcomb's Bennington College study. (560)

8. Define reference group. Give two reasons why people adopt reference-group attitudes. Why is such change more than superficial? (560)

9. *BOX 1:* Describe Asch's conformity studies. (562)

10. *BOX 1:* Define groupthink. What are the effects of groupthink? (563)

11. What happened to the Bennington students who remained conservative? In what way do social groups support attitudes? (561)

12. Describe Newcomb's follow-up study. What is the relationship between reference group selection and support for attitudes? How are the three foundations of attitudes related? (562)

CHANGING ATTITUDES

13. *BOX 2:* Define brainwashing. Describe the two phases involved. What did Schein find about the difficulty of brainwashing? (564)

14. Identify Carl Hovland. List the four components of a persuasive appeal. Describe the method used to study the effects of the communicator on attitude change. (564)

15. What are the two components of communicator credibility? Describe the effect of overheard communications. (564)

16. When is a one-sided message more effective? (566)

17. Describe the experiment by Janis and Feshbach. What conclusions were drawn from this experiment? (567)

18. What is the recent conclusion on fear appeals? What two conditions must be met for fear appeals to be effective? (567)

19. How is persuasion related to self-esteem? Describe the Janis and Mann study. What principle does it illustrate? Note two other examples of this principle. (568)

20. When are written messages and face-to-face or TV messages more effective? Describe the Chaikin and Eagly experiment. (569)

ATTITUDES AND BEHAVIOR

21. How consistent are attitudes and behavior? Explain how the link goes in both directions. (570)

22. What follows from making a statement you don't agree with? How does cognitive dissonance theory explain this situation? (570)

23. Describe the method, results, and conclusions of Festinger and Carlsmith's experiment. (571)

24. *BOX 3:* How does cognitive dissonance theory lead to the predictions Aronson made about residents around the Three Mile Island incident? What did a survey show? (572)

25. Describe Bem's self-perception theory and show how it explains the tendency for behavior to affect attitudes. What are the limits of the theory? (571)

OBEDIENCE TO AUTHORITY

26. Describe the subjects, setting, method, procedure, and results of Milgram's studies. (573)

27. Define the concept of legitimate authority. What do Milgram's results suggest about legitimate authority? (575)

28. Describe Milgram's study in which group pressure caused disobedience. What is the relationship between attitudes and situations? (577)

PSYCHOLOGICAL ISSUE: *PREJUDICE AND RACISM*

29. Distinguish among the terms racism, prejudice, and discrimination. Contrast the conclusions from surveys of racial attitudes and experiments involving actual behavior. (580)

30. Describe the concept of stereotype. Define selective perception, and tell how it is illustrated by Duncan's experiment. (582)

31. Describe the characteristics of the authoritarian personality. Describe the role of social norms in prejudice. (582)

32. What social-psychological principle suggests the most effective way to reduce prejudice? How did self-esteem of children figure in the 1954 Supreme Court desegregation decision? What went wrong? (584)

33. Define equal-status contact. Why is it necessary? Show how the Jigsaw technique provides it. (585)

Self-Quiz

1. Psychologists who measure attitudes with fixed-response techniques sometimes use a combination of questions, because:
   a. attitudes are complex.
   b. fixed-response techniques are not as valid.
   c. fixed-response questions are difficult to analyze quantitatively.
   d. all of the above. (Study Question 2)

2. In Shomer and Centers's experiment, the male student showing the fewest male chauvinist responses on a questionnaire filled out the questionnaire in a room containing:
   a. all men.
   b. one woman and the rest men.
   c. half women and half men.
   d. all women except for the subject. (Study Question 4)

3. The more arguments we have to support an attitude:
   a. the deeper the vertical structure.
   b. the broader the horizontal structure.
   c. the more logical the attitude.
   d. the looser the syllogistic structure. (Study Question 6)

4. Groupthink:
   a. is a highly productive approach to problems.
   b. suppresses critical judgment.
   c. encourages the expression of individual doubt and dissent.
   d. is the tendency to form stereotypes. (Study Question 10)

5. Newcomb's study of Bennington women showed:
   a. those who were liberals in their college years tended to remain liberal.
   b. those who were liberals in their college years became conservatives as the years went by.
   c. we tend to adopt and retain the political attitudes of our parents.
   d. social groups have the power to suppress political views, but they do not change them. (Study Question 7 and 12)

6. Compared to a message delivered directly, one that is "overheard" tends to be:
a. more easily ignored.
b. more persuasive.
c. less persuasive.
d. none of the above. (Study Question 15)

7. Spoken persuasive messages are more effective than written messages when:
a. the message is complex.
b. the message is simple.
c. the message is overheard.
d. the communicator is credible. (Study Question 20)

8. In an experiment by Festinger on cognitive dissonance, which students claimed to enjoy a boring experiment the most?
a. The students who were paid $20 to tell someone else they liked the experiment.
b. The students who were forced to tell someone else they liked the experiment, using the threat of a lower grade if they didn't.
c. The students who were promised a lucrative summer job for telling someone else they enjoyed the experiment.
d. The students who were paid $1 for telling someone else they enjoyed the experiment. (Study Question 23)

9. Discrimination toward a group of people is defined as:
a. negative judgments of them.
b. acting toward them on the basis of negative ideas.
c. racism.
d. all of the above. (Study Question 29)

10. The personality type that tends to see people in terms of a power hierarchy is:
a. external control.
b. authoritarian.
c. hostile.
d. dependent. (Study Question 31)

Answers to Self-Quiz: 1.a 2.b 3.b 4.b 5.a 6.b 7.b 8.d 9.b 10.b

Programmed Review Unit

evaluate / **social**

1. Your attitudes are the ways in which you ________________ people, objects, and issues; as such, your attitudes play a major role in determining ________________ behavior. (554)

COMPONENTS OF ATTITUDES: THOUGHTS AND FEELINGS

beliefs

2. Thoughts (or ________________) are the cognitive component of

affective
act

attitudes, while feelings are the ________ component. People do not always ________ in accordance with their attitudes. (555)

MEASURING ATTITUDES

open-ended
quantitatively
fixed
arousal
create
situation

3. Attitudes may be measured through ________ questions, which allow the respondents to make any response, but are hard to analyze ________. Most attitude measurement devices make use of ________-response questions, in which the respondents are asked to select one of a given set of answers to a question. Physiological measures indicate ________ rather than attitudes. Questionnaires and opinion polls may sometimes ________ attitudes rather than simply measure them. Furthermore, people's expressed attitudes can be influenced by the specific ________ in which the interview or questionnaire is exhibited. (556)

WHERE DO ATTITUDES COME FROM?

emotional/cognitive
social
classically

4. Bem presents the three foundations of attitudes as being the ________, the ________, and the ________ foundations. If you experience tears when you hear the national anthem, you have probably been ________ conditioned. (557)

arguments
change

5. The broader the horizontal attitude—that is, the more ________ we have for it—the more resistant that attitude is to ________. (559)

reference
liberal
liberal

6. In Newcomb's (1965) terms, the college community became a positive or negative ________ group for many of the Bennington women, who generally became more politically ________ than their parents. Twenty-five years later the Bennington alumnae had ________ political attitudes. (562)

32 – 35
5
doubts
illusion

7. In Asch's (1951) study, subjects conformed to the false group consensus on about ________ percent of the trials. When just one of the confederates gave the right answer rather than going along with the majority, the amount of conformity declined to ________ percent. Janis' notion of groupthink refers to the tendency for members of a policy-making group to suppress all individual ________, creating an ________ of unanimity. (562)

CHANGING ATTITUDES

difficult
brainwashing
communicator
message/audience
medium/effective

8. It is relatively ________ to change a person's attitudes; accordingly ________ is extremely difficult to accomplish. Persuasion has four components: a ________ delivers a ________ to an ________ through a particular ________. The same message was more ________ when subjects thought it had been delivered by the more expert

credibility sincerity influence	communicator. The ________ of a source is a factor that television advertisers are especially concerned with. Besides expertise, a communicator's credibility is based on his ________; much of the time, we do not trust people who we know are trying to ________ us. (564)
more limits reduce	**9.** The one-sided message is ________ effective if your audience is predisposed to agree with you or if they don't know that there is an opposing point of view. For fear appeals to be effective, the fear must be kept within ________ and the audience must be given specific information about how to ________ the threat. (566)
low actively	**10.** People who have ________ self-esteem are easily influenced. The more ________ you can involve people in the attempt to persuade them, the more likely they are to be persuaded. (568)
Written television emotional politicians	**11.** ________ messages, especially if they are complex, are usually easier to understand than spoken or ________ messages, which are more likely to have an immediate ________ impact: these are principles understood and used by ________. (569)

ATTITUDES AND BEHAVIOR

follow conformity more behavior inconsistency	**12.** Favorable attitudes toward racial integration typically ________ actual desegregation. A person's views are likely to change to come into greater ________ with a statement he or she has made. Festinger and Carlsmith (1959) found that subjects who had told the \$1 lie believed their lie ________ than subjects who told a \$20 lie. According to Bem's (1972) self-perception theory we often infer our own and other people's attitudes by observing our and their ________; Bem differs from Festinger's belief that we have an inner motive to reduce ________. (571)
confirmed	**13.** The cognitive-dissonance-theory predictions were ________ by the survey of residents close to Three-Mile Island. (572)

OBEDIENCE TO AUTHORITY

65 shock college women legitimate good 10 situations	**14.** Fully ________ percent of the subjects in Milgram's (1963; 1974) experiment were obedient to the end, continuing to ________ the "learner" until they reached the maximum level on the generator. Experiments involving ________ students and ________ produced similar results. Milgram's results indicate that it is extremely difficult to defy an apparently ________ authority. Milgram also found that a disobedient person can set a ________ example, as shown by the finding that only ________ percent of the subjects went up to the highest shock level when other subjects publically defied the experimenter's orders. Milgram's experiments demonstrated that people's actions are sometimes influenced more strongly by the pressures of specific ________ than by their enduring attitudes. (575)

PSYCHOLOGICAL ISSUE: *PREJUDICE AND RACISM*

attitude
treatment
Prejudice
attitudes/discrimination

15. Racism is the differential ________________ toward and ________________ of individuals on the basis of their racial group membership. ________________ is the prejudgment of people on the basis of their group membership, and refers to negative ________________, unlike ________________, which refers to actions toward such groups on the basis of prejudicial ideas. (580)

positive
behavior

16. Surveys indicate that racial attitudes have steadily become more ________________ and tolerant in America. However, this is not completely supported by studies of whites' ________________ toward blacks. (580)

groups or categories
perception

17. If we responded to every person as an individual, and didn't use ________________ at all, we would be free of prejudice. In the phenomenon of selective ________________ we tend to focus on information that is consistent with our stereotypes. (581)

authoritarian
weak/strong
power
discipline
status
weaknesses
projection

18. Highly prejudiced people are likely to have ________________ personalities and tend to see the world as divided into people who are ________________ and people who are ________________. Such people tend to be ________________-oriented, come from families that stressed harsh ________________ and obedience, as well as being anxious about family ________________ and personal ________________. They are also likely to make use of the Freudian defense mechanism of ________________. (582)

have not
norms

19. White southerners ________________ scored higher than white northerners on measures of authoritarianism. Patterns of discrimination against blacks in the South have been mainly a result of conformity to historical social ________________. (583)

follow
interracial

20. The best way to reduce prejudice is to apply the principle that attitudes ________________ behavior, and for example, increase the number of ________________ contacts. (584)

increased
equal / jigsaw

21. Stephan (1978) found that desegregation ________________ the prejudice of whites toward blacks as often as the other way. To be effective, interracial contact must be between people who have ________________ status in the situation. The ________________ technique provides equal-status, cooperative interracial contact. (585)

Self-Quiz

1. What percent of the real subjects in the Asch experiment conformed to the false but unanimous group consensus?
a. 0 percent.
b. 5 percent.
c. 15 percent.
d. 35 percent.

2. When confederate subjects publicly defied the experimenter's orders in the Milgram experiment, what percent of the real subjects obeyed orders to deliver the maximum level of shock?

a. 0 percent.
b. 10 percent.
c. 45 percent.
d. 65 percent.

3. Which one of the following is not true?

a. The best way to reduce prejudice is to have interracial contacts.
b. Authoritarian personalities are most likely to use the defense mechanism of repression.
c. Authoritarian personalities tend to see people along the dimension of weak/strong.
d. Sixty-five percent of Milgram's subjects delivered the maximum shock to the stooges.

4. Which one of the following is not true?

a. If we know someone is trying to influence us, we tend to resist him.
b. Bennington seniors were more politically liberal than Bennington freshwomen.
c. Bennington alumnae had political conservative attitudes 25 years later.
d. Attitudes include both thoughts and feelings.

5. Which one of the following is not true?

a. People's expressed attitudes can be influenced by the situation.
b. The more arguments we have for an attitude the harder it is to change.
c. The first step in brainwashing is to give the prisoner a new set of relationships.
d. It is relatively difficult to change a person's attitudes.

6. Which one of the following is not true of Janis's notion of groupthink?

a. Members of a policy-making group suppress individual doubts.
b. There is an illusion of unanimity.
c. Groupthink may have led to the poorly conceived rescue mission of U.S. hostages in Iran.
d. Groupthink is especially likely in a group that has low morale.

7. Which one of the following is not true?

a. High-fear communications are more likely to cause us to change.
b. Fear appeals must be accompanied with ways for the audience to reduce the threat.
c. If we didn't use categories, we would be free of prejudices.
d. A person's views are likely to come into greater conformity with statements the person makes.

8. If you deal with a black person differently than you would deal with a white person, you are showing:

a. prejudice.
b. discrimination.

c. stereotypic behavior.
d. common sense.

9. Which one of the following is not true?
   a. Authoritarian people come from families that were concerned with status.
   b. Authoritarian people come from families that stressed harsh discipline.
   c. White southerners score higher than white northerners on measures of authoritarianism.
   d. Recently, there are signs of enhanced self-esteem among black children.

10. Prejudice is to discrimination as ________________ is to ________________.
   a. projection/repression
   b. affect/cognition.
   c. thought/deed.
   d. roles/stereotypes.

Answers: 1.d 2.b 3.b 4.c 5.c 6.d 7.a 8.b 9.c 10.c

Chapter 19

Social Relationships

NEEDING OTHERS

1. Define the need for social comparison. Describe the experiments of Schachter, and show how they illustrate social comparison. (586)

2. Describe the following terms, distinguishing between them: (588)

   Emotional attachments—

   Social ties—

3. Compare and contrast two kinds of loneliness. Distinguish loneliness from being alone. How prevalent is loneliness? What groups are most affected? (592)

PERCEIVING OTHERS

4. Define person perception. How does physical appearance influence person perception? (592)

5. *BOX 1:* Describe the Dion et al. experiment and its conclusions. How does beauty create self-fulfilling prophesies? (592)

6. *BOX 1:* List the advantages and disadvantages of physical beauty. (592)

7. Describe Kelley's experiment. How do reputations influence person perception? (594)

8. Define attribution processes. Why are such inferences important in forming impressions? (594)

9. What is the central conclusion from attribution research? How is it illustrated by reactions to Milgram's study and by the Jones and Harris experiment? (595)

10. Describe the difference between attribution to others and attribution to self. (594)

11. *BOX 2:* Describe Archer's Social Intelligence Test (SIT). What two groups of people were better readers of nonverbal cues? (596)

LIKING OTHERS

12. What is the most common problem or wish among high-school students? Describe the authors' economic perspective on liking. (596)

13. Define the principle of proximity. Give illustrations of it, and indicate its limits. (597)

14. What is the single most important determinant of liking? Summarize the different respects in which friends have been found to be similar. (598)

15. Summarize the research of Newcomb and Byrne. What principle does it illustrate? (599)

16. List five reasons for the effects of similarity on liking. (599)

17. Compare the roles of similarity and diversity in determining friendship. What do the authors conclude? (600)

LOVING OTHERS

18. List three psychological approaches to the study of love. (601)

19. *BOX 3:* Identify Senator Proxmire. What issues did he raise? List the arguments for and against his position. (600)

20. Describe Rubin's love scale and each of its three components. (602)

21. How did Rubin validate the love scale? (603)

22. Distinguish loving from liking. How do men and women differ in love for their same-sex friends? (604)

23. Give Freud's view on love and sex. Summarize the research by Dermer and Pyszczynski and by Peplau et al. (604)

24. *BOX 4:* List distinguishing features of sexually traditional, moderate, and liberal couples. How do they all reveal the double standard? (606)

LEAVING OTHERS

25. List three ways in which the romantic ideal does not correspond to reality. (605)

26. Summarize Rubin's findings concerning similarity and involvement as causes of the breaking up of relationships. (607)

27. When are college couples most likely to break up? List two explanations to these findings. (607)

28. How does breaking up affect each partner in a relationship? (608)

PSYCHOLOGICAL ISSUE: *MARRIAGE AND DIVORCE*

29. What are the current statistics for divorce and remarriage for men and women? List two factors that seem to have increased the divorce rate. (610)

30. Define empty shell marriage. What kinds of problems precede and follow divorce? (611)

31. What colonial attitudes toward marriage have persisted? What are the reasons for the continuing appeal of marriage? (612)

Self-Quiz

1. In Schachter's study of affiliation under stress, it was found that:
   a. anxious people always seek out others who are calm.
   b. people who are afraid want to be with somebody—anybody.
   c. the need to seek company depends on how fearful the person is.
   d. most people would just as soon be left alone when under stress. (Study Question 1)

2. The kind of loneliness that Robert Weiss calls emotional isolation results from:
   a. the absence of emotional attachment.
   b. the loss of social ties.
   c. psychopathology.
   d. both *a* and *b* above. (Study Question 3)

3. The attribution process refers to:
   a. explaining behavior in terms of causes.
   b. attaching labels to people.
   c. compiling a person's positive characteristics.
   d. the principle of proximity. (Study Question 8)

4. The Social Intelligence Test (SIT) measures:
   a. ability to read nonverbal cues.
   b. knowledge of current events.
   c. sensitivity to social problems.
   d. skill in getting along with others. (Study Question 11)

5. In a survey of American high-school students, the most common wish expressed was:
   a. to achieve an identity.
   b. to be liked more.
   c. to be loved by someone special.
   d. to be more physically attractive. (Study Question 12)

6. The most critical similarities for friendship seem to be:
   a. physical characteristics.
   b. personality characteristics.

c. attitudes and beliefs.
d. social status. (Study Question 14)

7. In his study of love, Rubin found that:
a. men love their friends more than women do.
b. women tend to channel their love into a single opposite-sex relationship rather than into other relationships, as well.
c. love scales are not sensitive to platonic friendships.
d. women's relationships with others tend to be more intimate than are men's. (Study Question 22)

8. Peplau et al. found that premarital sex:
a. increased the chances of a couple staying together.
b. does not affect feelings of love in men or women.
c. has no effect on the longevity of a relationship.
d. is still quite rare, contrary to popular opinion. (Study Question 23)

9. Rubin and his coworkers found that couples are likely to break up:
a. if one partner is more involved in the relationship.
b. if they are too similar to each other.
c. if both partners are strongly involved in the relationship from the start.
d. none of the above. (Study Question 26)

10. Data on divorce show that:
a. over three-fourths of marriages will end in divorce.
b. more men remarry than women.
c. more women remarry than men.
d. most divorced people experience a great relief when the divorce is finally accomplished. (Study Questions 29, 30)

Answers to Self-Quiz: 1.c 2.a 3.a 4.a 5.b 6.c 7.d 8.c 9.a 10.b

Programmed Review Unit

NEEDING OTHERS

compare/two-thirds
one-third
similar

1. One of the main reasons we seek the company of others is to be able to ________ emotions and attitudes. Fully ________ of the high-fear subjects chose to wait with others compared to only ________ of the low-fear subjects. Schachter (1959) found that fearful subjects only wanted to wait with other people who were in a ________ situation. (587)

emotional
friends
loneliness/Isolation
restlessness/depression

2. Weiss (1974) believes that each of us needs ________ attachments to one other person and social ties to a network of ________. When people lack one or the other, the outcome is ________. ________ can be either social or emotional, and in either case may be painful, including symptoms of ________ and ________. One sort of relationship

cannot	________ readily substitute for another in alleviating
is not	loneliness. Being lonely ________ the same as being alone;
no more	people who live alone by choice are ________ likely to be
	lonely than people who live with others. In a 1969 national survey
26	________ percent of those interviewed had felt "very lonely
	or remote from other people" within the previous few weeks. (588)

PERCEIVING OTHERS

inferences	**3.** Person perception is the process of forming ________ about
	other people. Students who had been told that the graduate student was
warm	________ rated him as more considerate, sociable,
humorous	good-natured, and ________, even though he behaved no
	differently than he did for the students who had been told he was
cold/56	________. Also, ________ percent of the "warm"
	subjects took part in class discussions, as compared to 32 percent of the
	cold subjects. (594)
	4. Better-looking people are rated as being more sensitive,
kind/sociable	________, interesting, poised, and ________. They
	were also believed to have a greater chance of achieving success in their
careers/spouses	________, becoming good ________, and finding
happiness	________ in their lives. Teachers assumed that attractive
intelligent	children were more ________. Physical beauty seems to be
men	just as much of an advantage for ________. Attractive people
confident/fluently	are more self-________, speak more ________, and
persuasive	are more ________, on the average. (592)
overestimate	**5.** People have a tendency to ________ the degree to which other
	people's behavior is caused by their individual traits or disposition, and to
underestimate	________ the extent to which it is caused by
situational/more	________ factors. Interestingly, we are ________
	likely to attribute our own behavior to situational factors. (595)
	6. The most common problem or wish listed by American high-school
like	students in a 1958 survey was "I want people to ________ me
	more." We tend to like people who provide us with the greatest possible
rewards/cost	________ at the least possible ________. (596)
types	**7.** Videotapes can provide ________ of information that words
	cannot. For example, holding a baby gingerly is correctly interpreted as
unfamiliarity/Women	indicating ________ with the baby. ________ and
	parents of small children are better at reading nonverbal cues. (596)
proximity	**8.** Physical ________ is likely to bring us rewards at low
	cost. (597)
	9. The single factor that plays the largest role in determining whether we
similar	will like each other is how ________ we are, which is
attitudes	particularly true in our beliefs and ________. (598)
Agreement	**10.** ________ may provide a basis for engaging in joint activities,
confidence	for increasing our ________ in our opinions (which, in turn,
self-esteem	raises our ________), for making it easier to
communicate	________ with others, and for increasing the likelihood that
like	we will ________ each other. We are sometimes attracted to
different	people who are ________ from ourselves, especially if those

perspective

people give us a fresh ________ that we would like to learn more about. (599)

LOVING OTHERS

love
attachment/caring
intimacy
presence/emotional
responsibility
communication
eye

11. Psychologists have been slower to study the topic of ________. As defined in Rubin's (1970, 1973) scale, love consists of three components: ________, ________, and ________. *Attachment* refers to our need for the physical ________ and ________ support of the other person; *caring* refers to people's feelings of concern and ________ for another person; and *intimacy* refers to people's desire for close and confidential ________ with another person. Couples whose members had above-average scores on the love scale made significantly more ________ contact. (602)

favorable
married
lower
same-sexed
intimate
spontaneous
confidences

12. Liking, according to Rubin, refers to having a ________ evaluation of another person. Love scores were highly correlated with people's estimates of the likelihood that they would get ________; the correlation between liking scores and marriage likelihood were ________. When compared to men, women reported having more love but the same amount of liking for ________ friends; Caldwell and Peplau (1981) found that women's friendships tend to be more ________ than men's, involving more ________ joint activities and more exchanging of ________. (604)

increase
values
sexual intercourse
future

13. Dermer and Pyszczynski (1978) found that sexual arousal was likely to ________ male college students' love for their girlfriends. However, the link between love and sex is likely to depend on the sexual ________ of the people involved; Peplau, Rubin, and Hill (1977) found that whether or not a couple had ________ had no systematic effect on their ________ relationship. (604)

emotional

14. Whether a couple is sexually traditional, moderate, or liberal seems to be related to the link they see between sexual intimacy and ________ intimacy. (606)

LEAVING OTHERS

similar
half
age
career
attractiveness
differences/sexual
23

15. The large majority of love relationships and marriages are between people who come from highly ________ social backgrounds. Over a two-year period, about ________ of the couples in the Hill, Rubin, and Peplau (1976) sample stayed together, and were couples who tended to be more similar to one another in ________, intelligence, ________ plans, and physical ________. Couples who parted frequently mentioned ________ in interests, backgrounds, ________ attitudes, and ideas about marriage. Of the couples in which both members initially reported that they were equally involved in the relationship, only ________ percent broke up, while those couples in which one partner was more involved than the other had

Answers	
54 school vacations marriage	________ percent break-up. Separations of college students were more likely to take place when the ________ year is beginning or ending or during ________. Break-ups are most valuable if they take place before ________. (607)

PSYCHOLOGICAL ISSUE: *MARRIAGE AND DIVORCE*

Answers	
double 40 80 90	**16.** The American divorce rate by 1977 was ________ that of a decade earlier, and it is now estimated that about ________ percent of recent American marriages will end in divorce. About ________ percent of Americans who divorce eventually remarry, and over ________ percent of Americans marry at least once. (610)
forever happiness laws	**17.** Of all the possible factors for the increase in divorce rates, two seem to have had the greatest impact: 1) there seems to have been a gradual shift in values from the notion that marriage is ________, for better or for worse, to the notion that personal ________ and self-realization are the most important goals of individuals; and 2) this shift in values has been accompanied by changes in ________ that make it much easier than it used to be to end a marriage. (610)
physical	**18.** Divorce increases people's susceptibility to both psychological and ________ disorders. (611)
two and four years	**19.** Weiss (1975) found that it usually takes a divorced person between ________ to recover fully from the distress produced by the break-up. (611)
higher educational	**20.** There is evidence that single women tend to have ________ levels of intelligence, ________ and occupational status than married women. (613)
later/94 similar security sex children parents/tradition fluctuations/attraction	**21.** In recent years there has been a clear trend to getting married at a ________ age. In a 1980 poll of women, ________ percent said they favored marriage as a way of life; men show ________ views. The continuing appeal of marriage is based on, among other things, love, the desire for ________, the desire for ________ on a regular basis, the desire to have ________, the desire to "make it legal," pressure from ________, and the force of ________. Marriage serves to keep people together even in the face of temporary ________ in their feelings of ________ for one another. (613)

Self-Quiz

1. What proportion of marriages now taking place in the United States will probably end in divorce?

a. 10 percent.
b. 20 percent.
c. 30 percent.
d. 40 percent.

2. Which statement is not true of marriage and divorce?
   a. In 1977 the American divorce rate was double that of a decade earlier.
   b. Divorce increases people's susceptibility to physical disorders.
   c. It usually takes a divorced person between two and four months to fully recover from the break-up.
   d. Single women tend to have higher levels of intelligence and educational and occupational status than married women.

3. Compared with ________________ of the low-fear subjects who chose to wait with others, two-thirds of the high-fear subjects chose to wait with others.
   a. one-sixth
   b. one-third
   c. one-half
   d. two-thirds

4. When told that a graduate student teacher was warm, 56 percent of the students entered into class discussions with him, as compared to ________________ of the students who had been told that the graduate student was cold.
   a. 10 percent
   b. 32 percent
   c. 48 percent
   d. 56 percent

5. Which one of the following statements is not true?
   a. The double standard was uninfluenced by Freud.
   b. Approximately 78 percent of Americans marry at least once.
   c. Couples who parted cited differences in backgrounds, interests, and sexual attitudes.
   d. The increased divorce rate may be the result of an increased orientation to personal happiness and self-realization.

6. Which one of the following statements is not true?
   a. Men expressed more love than women for same-sexed friends.
   b. Couples with above-average love scores had more eye contact.
   c. Intimacy refers to close communication.
   d. Caring refers to responsibility.

7. Which one of the following statements is not true?
   a. We have a tendency to overestimate the extent to which other people's behavior is caused by situational factors.
   b. We are more likely to attribute our own behavior to situational factors than to our traits or disposition.
   c. We like people who provide us with the greatest possible rewards at the least possible cost.
   d. Close contact more often leads to liking than to disliking.

8. The similarities of most interest to us in deciding whether we will like another person is in our:
   a. age.

b. attitudes.
c. physical appearance.
d. level of intelligence.

9. Which one of the following statements is not true?
a. 1958 high-school students wanted most of all for people to like them more.
b. Twenty-six percent of Americans in a 1969 survey said that they had felt very lonely within the previous few weeks.
c. The single factor that plays the largest role in determining whether we will like each other is our proximity.
d. Rubin's love scale did not measure sexual attraction.

10. Which one of the following statements is not true?
a. We often seek the company of others to compare emotions and attitudes.
b. Weiss believes that we need an emotional attachment to another person.
c. Weiss believes that we need social ties to a network of friends.
d. Schachter found that people preferred to wait with others who were in a different situation.

Answers: 1.d 2.c 3.b 4.b 5.b 6.a 7.a 8.b 9.c 10.d

81 82 83 84 9 8 7 6 5 4 3 2 1